Praise for *Someone to Watch Over You*

"*Someone to Watch Over You* is a book about resilience. It's about becoming a stronger, more compassionate human being who embraces relationships and has the tools to weather life's challenges and find joy in each day. Ellen Reed walks beside you as you recover from adversity and become adept at facing the circumstances life puts before you. She's a coach and a guide who helps you grow as a person. This is an outstanding book, which should be on everyone's reading list, especially in these unpredictable times. You'll become a better version of yourself as you put her words into action."
— *Sharon J. Sherman, EdD, author, professor, and former dean of the College of Education and Human Services at Rider University*

"*Someone to Watch Over You* is an absolutely wonderful book that helps the reader find their inner self. This book is Ellen Reed's gift to all of us so that we may uncover hidden aspects of ourselves to develop rich relationships. This book assimilates the work of a variety of well-known therapists toward that end. It is easy to read. Each chapter presents a methodology to help us lead a more fulfilling life. She repeatedly reminds us that self-reliance is paramount in attaining fulfillment. She shows that we all have the ability to grow, change, and find strength to heal after adversity and loss. Ellen teaches us to believe in ourselves and fill our lives with loving people. She has spent her entire life showing kindness, appreciation, and love to everyone who knows her. I am proud to call her my mentor. She has made a real difference in the lives of so many."
—*Pamela Kance Brolin, MA, PMHCNS-BC*

"I am pleased to provide my sincere recommendations for Ellen Reed on the occasion of the completion of her book: *Someone to Watch Over You*. I had the pleasure to work with Ellen at Robert Wood Johnson University Hospital when she held the role of psychiatric clinical nurse specialist-consultation/liaison. As nursing director of Surgical Intensive Care Services, I frequently called on Ellen to provide intervention to our families, nurses, and physicians involved in the care of patients experiencing trauma or devastating illnesses. Ellen prepared families when conditions changed and death was imminent. Our chief of surgery asked his surgical residents to deliver bad news to family only when Ellen could be at their side. Ellen's book adds to a wealth of information on subjects that are critical for us all to learn and incorporate in our personal and professional lives."
—*Joanne Ritter-Teitel, PhD, RN, NEA-BC, chief nursing officer and associate dean of Clinical Practice, College of Nursing, at University Hospital of Brooklyn*

"After my second miscarriage, I was trying for two years for one last attempt at pregnancy with no luck. After entering therapy with Ellen, she made me realize my despair was tied to unresolved feelings over my dad's death. A simple suggestion to write my dad a letter and read it at his grave led to the weight of the world being lifted from me. Two months later I got my third attempt. I'm forever grateful to Ellen. I hope this book is a smashing success. If it helps others as much as Ellen helped me, there will be a lot of very grateful people in this world."
 —*J.G., therapy client*

"In *Someone to Watch Over You*, Ellen Reed takes an honest look at how we form our ideals and ways we can evolve. The road to self-discovery may have you questioning your beliefs and what led you to them, but you will come out of it with a greater understanding and sense of self. Her insightful stories and exercises offer an introspective look at personal growth that's especially relevant during this time of uncertainty."
 —*Julie Simon Fries, BA, MA, news executive, Sinclair Broadcast Group*

"I worked with Ellen when Baptist Medical Center, San Antonio, updated and standardized all clinical documentation into a new electronic format. Ellen provided a model of implementation and adoption that was easy to follow and learn. Ellen's passion for helping others was evident in her interactions with the hospital's administrative team, physicians, and clinical staff alike. The knowledge Ellen shared with me and my colleagues has been invaluable and translatable from work into my personal life and for that I am forever grateful. There is no way I can express all the gratitude and respect I have for her in a few sentences. I appreciate all the love and support she poured into me all those years ago."
 —*Sabrina Koog, DNP, MSN*

"*Someone to Watch Over You* is a must-read for global audiences. The book provides a framework and strategies to empower the reader through the skillful methodology of introspection. I met the author a decade ago, at a time in my life when I faced professional and intellectual challenges that were perceived as daunting, to say the least. Ellen's perspective, compassion, and skill elevated me from a world of trepidation, ambiguity, and uncertainty into a focused, empowered, self-aware individual who had purpose and obtained a clear understanding of the endgame in relation to my goals and aspirations in life. She taught me that love was the most powerful force in changing behaviors of individuals, groups, communities, and populations. In her model of interaction, love is the catalyst for all change—no matter how difficult the transformation. This book is a testament to the level of expertise she has in the field of clinical psychology and the experience she has in successfully facilitating change management in groups as well as individuals. I will use this book to teach my students, interns, and mentees on the values and attributes to live their best lives as well as encourage others to take a careful look at the context and qualitative value in this book, and how it will improve the quality of the lives we live."

—*Charles T. Folsom, Jr., RN, BSN, MSHA, senior industry best practice advisor, National Coordination Center*

"Ellen Reed writes a book that is full of clinical knowledge, wisdom, experience, and full of personal anecdotes that shows she has put her vast studies into practical use. Far more than a self-help book, *Someone to Watch Over You* gives solid insights into how life can be lived in a healthy and joyful way, and she does that by introducing many and varied tools, examples, and exercises. It is about becoming fully and deeply human—warts and all. Knowing Ellen, it comes from her depth of spirituality and connection with God. It is what she wishes for you as well."

— *Reverend Doctor Joel G. Hafer*

Someone to Watch Over You
Finding your strength within

Ellen J. Reed
MBA, MSN, RN, PMHCNS-BC

Paraclete Publications

Paraclete Publications
Flat Rock, North Carolina
ellenreed215@gmail.com
www.EllenJReed.com

Copyright © 2020 by Ellen J. Reed
All rights reserved. This book may not be reproduced in whole or in part, stored in a retrieval system, or transmitted in any form or means—electronic, mechanical or other—without written permission from the publisher, except by a reviewer who may quote brief passages in a review.

The material in this book is intended for education. It is not meant to take the place of diagnosis and treatment by a qualified medical practitioner or therapist. No expressed or implied guarantee of the effects of the use of the recommendations can be given or liability taken.

Book Cover Art: The book cover represents "Beautiful Soul," which was generously gifted by artist Laurie Shiparski (Laurie Authier Art) as we follow each other's plan to help others grow.

Lead Editor: Jordan Parker Reed
Consultant: Shelley Lieber
Editor: Cinda Adams Gaskin

Book Cover and Text Design: Janet Aiossa

First Printing: May 2020
ISBN 978-1-7348405-0-6
Ebook ISBN 978-1-7348405-1-3

Some names and identifying details have been changed to protect the privacy of individuals.

Printed in the United States of America as an environmentally minded publication under the auspices of E. Reed Enterprises, LLC.

Someone to Watch Over You
Finding your strength within

To George,
my best and dearest friend and husband,
my sons Christopher and Michael,
my educators, and God—all who taught me
what it was to believe.

Contents

Intent | vii

Who Should Read This Book | ix

Chapter 1: The Building of Self | 1

Chapter 2: There's a Place for Us | 23

Chapter 3: We Are Family | 39

Chapter 4: I Want to Be Somebody | 57

Chapter 5: It's All About Love | 77

Chapter 6: Finding the Words to Say | 95

Chapter 7: On Grieving | 117

Chapter 8: The Path of Resilience | 139

Chapter 9: It's Just the Beginning | 157

My Many Thanks | 172

About the Author | 174

Notes | 176

Recommended Reading | 179

Intent

Each of us faces struggles in life that can generate a level of unrest, or even crisis. Though most of us share a strong cultural value to be independent, there are times in all of our lives when we need somebody. *Someone to Watch Over You* offers you the opportunity to appreciate your *self* and your ability to be resilient through life's most difficult challenges. It encourages relationships that serve you and acceptance of the reality of loss when they do not.

This book serves as a tool of sorts, supporting you as you adapt a new perspective that will improve the way you deal with challenges. *Someone to Watch Over You* upholds a legacy of finding value and worth in yourself and in others. If you believe, as I do, that meaningful change can come out of kindness and understanding, and that some of the worst situations can produce personal growth, this book will solidify those beliefs and empower you to significantly enrich your life and the love you give and receive.

I wrote this book as an extension of my 34 years as a therapist, supporting individuals facing new realities or life changes, those who have been deeply troubled by loss, and those who were facing death. And during my 14 years as an organizational consultant and project manager supporting healthcare corporations, I have assisted countless employees in navigating corporate life, processing change management, and building communication skills necessary to be resilient and to achieve success during their careers.

Similarly, I'm here to serve you by helping you to discover new levels of your own personal strength through self-acceptance, embracing supportive relationships, and mastering resilience. There is a Greek word, Παρακλετος (Parakletos), that means "one who moves close beside." It describes one who serves as a loving presence, a helper, a counselor, a comforter, and an advocate.[1] I give myself as a Paraclete to you through the pages of this book, as I count it a privilege to walk beside you as you grow through this season and upcoming seasons of your life.

Who Should Read This Book?

Throughout my life journey as a nurse, a Gestalt therapist, and later a consultant, I realized that many capable and successful individuals struggle through life and at times enter into crisis when faced with stressors beyond their control. Stress, to the degree of crisis, occurs when we lack the internal resources to define and master a problem, or at least, refuse to reach acceptance of a destiny presented before us. Another layer to this is whether our struggle has a solution and is fixable, or whether it is an ongoing process—a polarity[2]—about which we need to learn to manage.

Lacking self-awareness to accommodate stress, along with lacking the assistance of adequate support, can impact individuals, families, and groups as they instinctively attempt to cope.

> Stress, to the degree of crisis, occurs when we lack the internal resources to define and master a problem, or at least, refuse to reach acceptance.

Many individuals have diminished coping or have engaged in lower level coping/defense measures, which may help temporarily but may also create additional problems. Turning to alcohol and drugs to deaden pain is a clear example. So many people walk through life with a veil of sadness and hopelessness following their every step. People do not want to hurt, either physically or emotionally, and so what may seem like an obvious solution can complicate circumstances.

Generally requiring risk and courage, advocates of communication recognize that crucial conversations can stimulate health, but these conversations can also serve as a catalyst for immediate change. There is a delicate balance among human behaviors. As you engage in any relationship, being a solid communicator is the right thing to do.

In this book, you will learn to communicate both your thoughts and feelings in a timely manner so that the person you are addressing has a better understanding of the intent. However, you will need to be prepared for the responses you may receive.

Consider these questions that can impact our behavior:

Do I clearly state my discontent and set in motion behavior on the part of another?

If I say what is truly bothering me, will I be abandoned and experience further loss when my hope was to open lines of communication and resolution?

And so, it becomes important never to remove coping mechanisms that serve individuals or groups before introducing more substantial, healthier choices.

Of greatest concern are desperate people who see no way to resolve problems with civility. Instead, they become lethal and resort to irrational thinking, believing they are justified in hurting or even killing others. Others may avoid commitment or hold unfair expectations while failing to address their own behavior. Avoidance of thoughts and feelings of fear, loneliness, actual or anticipatory loss, abandonment, and failure can create incredible instability and the need for intervention. While thoughts affect emotions, and emotions influence our actions, loss promotes fear-based living, which often paralyzes individuals and sometimes the environment [culture and people] in which they live to the point of instability and apathy.

Someone to Watch Over You is my humble effort to put into words a lifetime advocacy that supports individuals and groups taking a (sometimes) difficult journey of introspection. Through my years of experience serving as a therapist and consultant, I hope to educate readers on the importance of improving self-awareness, discovering what makes you unique, and helping you to consider the person you want to be. This book recognizes the work that needs to be done in order to change and encourages soul-searching, whether change is worth it to you now or in the future.

You might benefit from this book if you are struggling with crisis or loss or have a general sense of disappointment that life is not going as expected. The pain of grief can manifest from many life situations which are experienced as a loss. Although generally viewed as the loss of a person, grief and loss can occur during any disruption in homeostasis. Homeostasis is defined as a mechanism of the body to maintain a stable internal environment despite changes occurring in the external environment. This effort occurs on a psychological and physical level. Thus, grief can be experienced by a divorce, the loss of a job, or even broken dreams.

Homeostasis is defined as a mechanism of the body to maintain a stable internal environment despite changes occurring in the external environment. This effort occurs on a psychological and physical level.

In an attempt to cope, many of you may skillfully try to avoid the feeling and pain of grief. Especially in the case where there are multiple competing stressors like work or caring for others, the priority may be to just get through each day. When conflict is too uncomfortable, the instinct is to "turn the page," and avoid the source of pain. The result is the creation of an unresolved griever who, at some unsuspecting time later in life, will feel the pain they attempted to avoid. This time, it may be an accumulation of grief that is overwhelming and totally unmanageable.

For those more fortunate, this disruption is sometimes enough to cause an awakening, a time of questioning, and an emergence from a previous state of resistance and denial. This time offers a "foot in the door" for change. While crisis creates a sense of vulnerability, it also allows individuals a time to reflect on alternatives they previously had not considered.

Do you see yourself in any of these questions?

- Do you wake up with sadness?
- Are you searching for your life's meaning and purpose?
- Do you have a problem to solve or a polarity to manage? Do you believe the problem to be unsolvable?
- Are you afraid that once you speak your truth, actions will occur that will inevitably end a relationship?
- Have you identified the values and beliefs you hold important in yourself and others?

- Have you had an experience with loss of any kind?
- Has someone presented you with a life-changing diagnosis?
- Has there been a death of a family member, a friend, a pet, a spouse?
- Did you lose your job, an ideal, or a dream for your future?
- Are you struggling with infertility or have had a pregnancy loss?
- Do you have unresolved issues with someone and are unable to communicate these, or resolve the hurt?
- Have you recently retired and are struggling to understand your worth and your 'new normal'?
- Are you afraid to love and commit to another person?
- Are you experiencing blame and shame?
- Has a member of your immediate social circle disappeared from your life?
- Have you attempted to avoid the pain of grief?

It is my hope that persons needing to change and/or those who wish to offer support, benefit from the wisdom set forth in the content of this book.

1

The Building of Self

If you are reading this book, it is likely that you have a strong desire to correct an experience that has raised distress and apprehension about the way you are proceeding through life, your response to a present condition, or your reaction to an event that keeps replaying in your mind. You may have experienced loss and are holding on by your fingertips, hoping that sadness will be replaced by joy and that you can feel whole again. You might even have used anger to keep away any threats, as emotions are often used to serve as a protection.

You have a hunch that life could be better and that perhaps something is missing that could help you. And while you know things are not going as you imagined, you can't seem to find a better solution. You may have set into motion a series of self-fulfilling prophecies by believing something about yourself that has no merit in your reality. These unfounded beliefs sometimes become reinforced to the degree that they become the foundation by which you plan your life. You may be ready to take a step back to better understand, "How did I get here, and what can I do to improve the way I feel?"

Someone to Watch Over You can offer insight into reaching a better understanding about the person you have become. Throughout the book, you will be encouraged to examine your contribution to every relationship, uncover any need to rebuild support, and help you reclaim the person you want to be. By acknowledging your thoughts and feelings, learning how to assess your current state, and applying that which you find useful as you read through these pages, the intent is to help you connect the dots and get you on the path to improving your life.

Walk into any doctor's office, and it's likely that a staff member will ask you to fill out an exhaustive review of your body's systems—from your brain to your GI tract. You carefully fill out the form describing your medical history: Surgeries, illnesses, medications you're currently taking, and treatments you have had.

If you are seeking legal advice, a similar process occurs. The attorney will ask you to describe, in your own words, the reason for your visit and what you hope will happen as a result of the interaction.

Similarly, as you read this book, I am asking you to organize any facts that will help you better understand your current state of being. What happened in your past and what is happening now? What would you like to see happening in the future? And at the very least, what do you imagine will happen if you do nothing to change?

Let's agree that you are the expert on the topic of *you*. You know yourself better than anyone else. You are the one who controls your past, your history, and any memories that you care to remember and act upon in your life. You already know what precipitated your search for this book today. Has something changed that raises your concern?

In the past, you followed your intuition and instinctively worked toward meeting your own needs. It's likely that you've done an exceptional job of taking care of yourself. However, any one of us can experience a situation or a time in our lives that requires a different plan of action. You may be facing a crisis and are not prepared to deal with the magnitude of stress. Your resources, those things you have always called on to calm a situation, may no longer be working for you.

In the way that people seek help to get out of debt, you're seeking a solution to a problem that requires new skills. In a similar manner, one by one, you may need to reevaluate or eliminate items from your script that hold opinions, attitudes, and beliefs given to you along the way and replace them with those that you have developed on your own. It may be time to only keep the ones that serve you. My goal is to assist you in finding yourself, reclaiming your identity, and discovering who you are and who you want to be. This describes the complex process of *individuation*.

Chapter 1: The Building of Self

Understanding Individuation

In coming into the world, a great deal of energy is spent being part of a family and establishing relationships with a mother, father, siblings, and other prominent family members. *Individuation* is the psychological phase of separating from a long list of behaviors and beliefs and defining oneself as an individual with one's own sense of *self*. *Individuation* is the act of self-realization. This process is part of the development of a healthy, functioning personality as each of us embraces and defines our uniqueness based on several conscious and unconscious factors.

Generally, beliefs that we have internalized begin at home but can also occur in church, school, work, or within any setting where there are people in authority. It may be helpful for you to read some actual examples from situations when those involved needed to process experiences that were getting in their way.

For example, take my situation in high school: As a highly motivated Advanced Placement high school student, I struggled with a physics exercise to create a sample of an electric circuit. Each time I tried, my board blew a fuse. Instead of explaining what I might be doing wrong, the physics teacher expressed his frustration by projecting blame. After the third time, he yelled across the classroom, "Ellen, you are never going to amount to anything!" Whether he meant to or not, he publicly created a new reality for me. For years, his words resounded each time I was about to face an unfamiliar task. What was at stake was a life of self-doubt. I believed in the teacher's message, felt ashamed, and was unable to separate from the reality he had presented. Furthermore, the shame was reinforced by a classroom full of peers who innocently laughed as they were happy not to be the source of the teacher's scorn for that day. Fortunately, my family taught and lived by many virtues. I could hear my mother's message to always complete tasks and her gentle encouragement of, "If at first you don't succeed, try, try again."

I *did* try again and passed the AP Physics class. I graduated high school and went on to college, earning a Bachelor's degree in Nursing and later on started a Master's curriculum. It was years later, when assigned to be his nurse in a busy New York City emergency room, I was finally able to prove my physics teacher wrong. When he thanked me profusely for helping him, I reminded him of his statement and the potential effect it might have had. He actually admitted regret and added that he was quite pleased that I was there for him that day.

To a young impressionable student, his powerful remarks created a risk that could have become a reality for me. However, my personal beliefs and values helped overcome the teacher's negativity, and I succeeded.

Sometimes a message that shapes our beliefs about our *self* and others is masked in something that seems positive, such as "All the McCoy men in our family are successful professionals." What do you do with this if you are a McCoy man who has a desire to be an artist and who values success with a different measure? And what about the women in this family?

A rather animated undergraduate philosophy professor of mine once called out to his classroom full of students, "There are no absolutes." He was very clear in this conviction that absolute statements are not meant to describe human beings who, brimming with different talents and flaws, fill the world with excitement and discovery. He was doing all that he could to shape the minds of his students and help them understand that we needed to treat each person as an individual. This was a novel idea for the time as most of us still held tightly to the beliefs of our families and rarely had an original thought or plan.

It is ironic to me that highly capable people may operate based on events from the past or the past of others. However, we all do this to some degree. Beliefs that occurred during an earlier generation may remain and outlast their usefulness. For instance, take this statement: *"Children should be seen and not heard."* This proverb dates back to John Mirk's *Festial*, published by a clergyman around 1450. His intention was to reprimand young girls and celibate men who entered into adult conversation. The way of the world was clearly different in those times, yet the statement has lasted.

There are other examples of absolute statements that have lasted through the years:

"Don't count your chickens before they are hatched," a warning to avoid overestimating your assets or your abilities.

"Don't shoot the messenger," a metaphor for protecting the bearer of bad news.

"All Millennials lack a sense of loyalty," an explanation into the behavior of a newer generation. This too may be an incorrect generalization as I know four Millennials rather intimately and hardly believe that all Millennials lack a sense of commitment and loyalty.

Perhaps you can see that these and other absolute statements, particularly those that instill unnecessary fears, may remain as part of your truth without evidence of need. The unwinding and undoing of these old patterns of belief can be a source of great conflict. For example, if your mother experienced a man to be unfaithful, do you tend to expect this from all men coming into your life? These old belief systems may change your perception about people and influence your ability to be open to new relationships. A way to move beyond this is to set a new standard for yourself. Here again you must ask: Who do you want to be? Consider allowing yourself to treat people the way you want to be treated and not making conclusions before you have had a chance to observe or learn more about them.

Chapter 1: The Building of Self

In truth, no two people are alike. Yet when absolute statements are made to contrive wisdom, they not only stand in the way of reasonable judgement, but can create biases and prejudices that cause underlying fear. These statements are a window into old wounds that need to be healed and set aside.

Your effort toward *individuation* allows all of the cards to be placed on the table and choices determined based upon your humanity. Each of us has a unique set of characteristics based upon innate qualities, attitudes, values, virtues, beliefs, opinions, and experiences. We have adapted these traits and worked on them diligently, albeit sometimes unconsciously, in an effort to create an identity that will allow us to fit into the world. Beneath this individuality are far more commonalities among people that offer universal traits and needs, yet we are hardly the same.

Much like baby ducklings who are rooted to follow their mother in a single file to safely cross the street, we listen and watch intently to the people around us whom we instinctively trust in order to learn how to manage life. People are patterned to follow fixed ways of behaving in any given prescribed situation. We may use role models from our family or friends who are merely following what they learned from those before them. Without thought or discrimination, every day we find people repeating or copying the way others behave, the way they think, and how they act without bothering to ask why or consider the consequences. You may be aware of relationships where abuse, neglect, and abandonment are prominent themes. While the joy is hard to find, people stay in these relationships. Why? A possible answer is that they may have seen this pattern of abuse for generations and now almost expect this to be part of what's normal, unable to see that they deserve better.

Despite influence from others who can create an uncertain reality, it is quite possible to change and set in motion improvements to our condition. During *individuation*, a person accepts a responsibility and exhibits a willingness to become open to being different. This action may require the rewriting of old scripts to incorporate the qualities and beliefs that provide definition to the person you long to be. At times, it also requires a person to stand firmly on newly defined traits that may be quite alien to your family. Until an individual gets to the other side of the process of change, this can be a solitary experience. But once they arrive on that other side, there is great relief in finding their authentic self and living the life they choose. Once a person can state for sure who they are and how they want to live their life, they can rewrite absolute statements or whatever patterning has occurred and unite with other like-minded individuals.

"We can write and live our own scripts more than most people will acknowledge. I also know the price that must be paid. It's a real struggle to do it. It requires visualization and affirmation. It involves living a life of integrity, starting with making and keeping promises, until the whole human personality, the senses, the thinking, the feeling, and the intuition, are ultimately integrated and harmonized."[3]

—*Stephen R. Covey*

We must believe that no one ever chooses to do less than their best in making decisions in life. Our parents and their parents before them are included. However, the challenges faced by our ancestors may not be the same as ours today and their attempt to cope may not work as well or even be needed today. For instance, many of the events in our ancestors' lives touched upon safety and security issues. Perhaps we no longer have the same reason to walk through life afraid and anxious, yet we may still carry this anxiety and fear within us.

For example, my grandmother's way of coping was to sit for long hours in solitude and prayer. She faithfully recited the rosary, believing she would find the answers she needed as she chanted a different prayer for every bead. If she were alive today, she might be engaging in conversation and trying to better understand how she could take responsibility to resolve any one of her life's dilemmas.

Despite our best efforts, there are times when we fail to solve our problems or move forward successfully after a challenge. Clearly, we cannot just rely on how our parents or ancestors dealt with their problems to deal with our own. Without the knowledge, resources, or experience to overcome difficulties, our growth is woefully limited. Each of us is responsible and accountable for our own happiness and need to develop skills enabling growth that can overcome significant personal problems.

This may mean shedding old or outdated beliefs about yourself. Many times, it takes courage you didn't know you could find. It may require taking a chance to formulate new thinking. It may mean turning to a trusted advisor. At the very least, you must start to believe that you deserve better. It may be time to acknowledge that the anger you may be carrying is actually pain you've endured in the past and the fear you experience is a manifestation of past rejection.

Chapter 1: The Building of Self

In proceeding through life and relationships, no one ever chooses to do less than their very best. But when our very best fails to solve our problems or proceed with success, we need to seek other solutions.

Much like old baggage, many of us carry around a set of memories attached to feelings, a prominent one being the fear of loss. It may be that the fears we inherited from others now stop us from taking chances and trying new challenges. Take fear for example: Fear bubbles up to our awareness and presents as a physical change in our body, creating anxiety. That anxiety can present itself as a racing pulse or a sense of butterflies in our stomachs. Or, it may appear as jittery hands and feet. All of this is a behavioral representation of our feelings, likely fear, which we can learn to interpret as a warning.

But we may continue to carry fears about relationships not lasting or times when we were unsuccessful in meeting our needs. We may have a sense of confusion or discomfort about walking a path that is unfulfilling or unfamiliar. For many of us, avoidance and denial are our go-to coping mechanisms, leading us to move past the signs or red flags that something is not right with our world. We likely do so because we lack an instant solution to handle the situation, and so it becomes a habit to just move on, never resolving the source of our stress or anxiety. These measures only work for so long. What may be missing is a major step where we actually need to stop and take time to do a personal assessment:

Who am I?
What do I hold important to me?
What are my guiding principles?
What life lessons have I learned that help me cope?
Am I at peace?
How do I want to be perceived by others?
What brings me joy?
What life passages do I hold as important?
Have any of my dreams and accomplishments for life passed me by?
To whom do I find myself attracted?
What frightens me or makes me avoid certain circumstances?
What am I searching for?

These are only some of the characteristics that serve as a foundation of self-awareness. This introspective, *individuation* work is the first step to alert you to areas that need your attention. I encourage you to start paying attention, on a deeper level, to what you feel, along with your thoughts and physical reactions. To reach a sense of wholeness, it is important to join mind, body, and spiritual awareness so that you have the best advantage in fully knowing yourself. With practice, this ability becomes second nature. Once you are clear about who you are and any dissonance between your previous response to struggles and who you want to be, you have an opportunity to do something about it. The next time you face an uncomfortable or difficult situation, refrain from reacting on autopilot with denial or avoidance or whatever coping mechanism you lean on most. Instead, ask yourself:

How does this situation make me feel?
Where am I feeling my feelings?
Are there any memories of past events that are coming up right now?
What was my previous response and what impact did it have?
Am I having any thoughts that come to my awareness?

These questions are meant to provide you with a better understanding of yourself. Anything you do that allows you a better understanding of all parts of you will be a great advantage in negotiating the world. Sadly, many highly intellectualized people tend to explain their experience of life situations from their thoughts rather than integrating both their thoughts *and* feelings. They proceed through life like little heads being held up by the stress of the world in which they live. Essentially, they are disconnected from their feelings, a quite powerful part of the equation.

If you act this way, you may miss the whole of a situation and risk responding with your limited knowledge, using only some of the tools available to discern the world. Your observations are then based on "what I think," not on "what I think and feel."

When not fully in touch with the whole of our thoughts and feelings, we may unknowingly judge the world and people incorrectly.

Chapter 1: The Building of Self

Attached to every thought—and likely every object to which we are exposed—is a feeling. I encourage you to allow yourself to feel those feelings in order to capture the lessons to be learned about people, things, and events. Consider this: Say you're preparing to move to a different town or city, and the goal is to just get through each busy day, packing up as much as you can. As you pack your belongings, you may be tempted to just move past your feelings and quickly pack up the parts of you that represent your past. But much can be learned about yourself in these moments.

There have been many times when I have stopped packing boxes to review every letter, every saved card, or gift passed on by people of significance. I recall the times I moved and never quite finished the job of unpacking a box that I've coined as "Box No. 6." We were just one week away from the day our moving truck was due to arrive. I took off time from work to address all of the items that had been stored under our basement stairs for the 17 years we lived in our house. I found some of our first Christmas decorations, the paper ones that were safe to use when you have two toddlers in the house. Years of being in a musty basement meant they could be thrown away. There were also old textbooks that could be discarded since the information was clearly outdated and of no value to anyone else. And then there was Box No. 6.

Box No. 6 had become a running joke in our family because it hadn't been opened in years, and no one actually knew what was inside. We moved it from our apartment to our first house and then from state to state for many years. Box No. 6 had taken on a life of its own, but this time I was determined to reach an understanding and put an end to the joking.

Upon careful consideration, I realized that Box No. 6 represented something from my past—a time before I married my husband. It wasn't until I acknowledged the meaning and *feelings* attached to the contents of this box that I could disengage myself from the burden it had become and embrace the joy it was intended to provide.

When I finally opened Box No. 6, it contained a beautiful set of glassware that perfectly matched my dinnerware. It was a gift from my Godparents, who knew how much I admired their place settings each time they invited me to dinner. But

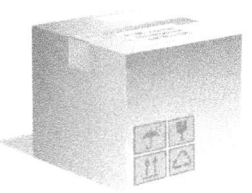

it represented much more than just lovely glassware. It represented a warm and secure relationship with two people who knew me and loved me as much as my parents. As Godparents, they were designated to be my parents should anything happen to my birth parents. Box No. 6 surely had greater depth and meaning than any of us imagined. Opening it was freeing and illuminating; it reminded me of a time when I was well-supported. It also helped me realize that I no longer needed to be cared for in this manner. To this day, I am unsure about all the reasons I may have avoided opening Box No. 6, but I believe that I wasn't yet prepared to let it go until then.

I share my experience and this illustration for you to consider areas that are unknown to you and ready to be explored. Less obvious are some of the feelings and attitudes inherited from generations past, especially those that may not even fit with the person you have become or want to be. As part of your search for understanding, there is great value in learning more about your beginning and your family's rich history. It may be an important time to collect facts from a variety of family members to learn more about who you are, and not only who you think you are.

> As part of your search for understanding, there is great value in learning more about your beginning and your family's rich history.

My Beginning

My mother was the only daughter of Italian immigrants who raised five children. My father was one of six children born to Russian and Polish parents, who arrived in America with a determination to make a better life for themselves and their progeny. My mother spoke no English until she went to school at age eight, and my father was only able to attend school through the sixth grade because he needed to work to support the family.

My grandparents must have been incredibly courageous and very open to change to be able to leave behind so many "knowns" of their respective rural villages in Europe to enter the world they found in New York City. No, the streets were not paved in gold in America as they had been told. The streets south of Houston Street—where they lived—provided a strong cultural beginning centered around church and job opportunities in the textile industry.

The Germans were the first to arrive in New York in the late 1800s, followed by Irish, Italians, Poles, Ukrainians, and other ethnic groups. Particularly interesting to my own historical roots was the arrival of the Italians from Southern Italy

Chapter 1: The Building of Self

and Jewish immigrants from Russia and Eastern Europe. The Jewish people and Italians worked and lived side by side, always aspiring for something better.

Hester Street in Little Italy

It is no surprise that in 1935, an Italian American woman and a Russian Jewish American man fell in love while working in a lady's garment factory. My father was the production manager. My mother was a forelady, working with the many women hired to sit at sewing machines finishing piece goods, which were part of an assembly line approach to fabricating clothing.

They married, despite the concerns of their parents. My Jewish grandmother threatened she would jump off the Brooklyn Bridge; my Italian grandmother feared my mother's excommunication from the Catholic Church. Neither of those things happened, and my family evolved because of the strength and courage this young couple exhibited. Their values quickly merged and they entered into a future characterized by hard work, education, and achievement.

My mother was a kind and loving woman who put her family first. My father, my hero, was a risk-taker and high achiever who showed us the value of being kind and respectful to all people with whom you interact. I watched him work with his leadership in New York's Garment District and with factory workers in rural Tennessee. He demonstrated the same respect for CEOs and those who were barely making minimum wage. When I had the occasion of walking by his side, men would stop him on Sixth Avenue to offer hugs and congratulations on a job well done. Similarly, the ladies in his Tennessee factories would giggle with joy upon his arrival to review their work.

Unfortunately, beyond many of their successes, fear remained as the most pronounced residual feeling of my parents' lives. My mother didn't realize how much the lack of safety experienced by her mother and other relatives as they arrived in America had imposed an overarching sense of fear that translated into my young life.

My grandmother's fear makes total sense to me now. The primary need for most humans is acceptance, and the number one fear is rejection.[4] My grandmother was a young woman when she crossed the ocean in steerage on a ship that was wall to wall people. I acknowledge that she must have been frightened at times during her passage and again at Ellis Island where she witnessed many individuals being refused entry into the United States. However, I also believe that her judgement, courage, and resilience were powerful forces to allow her to succeed. She decided to have faith that she was meant to make this change and did all that she could to make it successful for her children.

This is an incredibly important awareness for you as well. We all operate upon a mechanism whereby our thoughts affect our feelings and our feelings affect our behavior. Therefore, when a person feels threatened or frightened in their surroundings, a natural response is to protect or seek shelter. This protection comes in words and actions. For my mother, it was her "be careful" message. My mother had been fed this message from the time she was a baby, and she fed this same message to her children—and me—as we stepped outside to catch the bus for school. To the child within me, I imagined there was something ominous outside of the confines of my house.

Our Developmental Awareness: From Birth to Adulthood

Consider the image of a mother feeding her baby a spoonful of applesauce. Unfamiliar with what is being placed into her mouth, the baby resists and pushes the applesauce out with her tongue. But here it comes again, until the baby is forced to accept it. In much the same way, children take in messages without the ability to discriminate and often take on the history of generations before them.

Chapter 1: The Building of Self

They then end up acting upon that which is not their concern.

For every young child, walking, talking, feeding, pooping, and peeing are significant milestones, yet the basics of human survival also offer opportunities for social interaction and praise from our caretakers, whether they are the traditional or contemporary Mother/Father, Mother/Mother, Father/Father, and extended family or the Nanny/Babysitter or Childcare Worker. Boldly and without inhibition, our childlike self declares, "I did it." Hopefully the return response is filled with hugs and celebration to help reinforce these amazing accomplishments. Thus, we grow and develop based upon the feedback we receive and begin to appreciate the importance of being surrounded by loving people.

Not everyone is quite so fortunate to be born into a family that understands the need to nurture and support a growing individual. A child or adult develops their confidence in believing they are an exceptional addition to the world through sound feedback from people they admire and trust. When this gift is missing, one may seek approval from trusted sources and become their own best support system.

In his book *Notes to Myself: My Struggle to Be a Person*, Hugh Prather describes a belief that, "Anxiety is the tension between my desire to control the world and the recognition that I can't."[5] The development of anxiety can take many forms. It can become the message of "not good enough" or the "fear of failure" or "disappointment," leaving you to doubt your worth. Anxiety may come from one or more of the many messages that stand in the way of taking risks or exercising courage. The "not good enough" message makes you doubt even the most intelligent contributions you make. As a result of this rather common and powerful message, the child or adult tends to seek perfection in most everything they do. The anxiety may be exhibited in procrastination. It may be mistaken as being lazy or uncaring when it is, at a deeper level, a fear of rejection or disapproval.

Have you experienced tension rising within you when completing a project because you anticipate judgement and criticism? Many times, a person with a "not good enough" script holds back in reaching the end of a project or assignment. They spend considerable time tweaking their work instead of sending it forth. This same individual may opt out of requesting a promotion or accepting membership on committees, even though it's integral to the success of their work. In addition, they may decide that they are not worthy of being in a relationship and act this out by seeming to be uncaring.

Human developmental theorists present a wealth of knowledge around the events occurring as we grow from childhood to adolescence and into adulthood. Many people fail to consider who they are and think it is the result of a mere coincidence of nature, something ingrained in us and not open to choice and change. This is so far from reality. I believe there are no coincidences. Who we are and the qualities that make us who we are have been under construction for generations. However, the good news is that all of us, while proceeding in a unidirectional path from birth to death, are ever-evolving. We are adding new experiences that life offers and observing the success in which we handle every new challenge. Each of us has the ability to turn life around and to reach our personal achievements.

The Concept of Change

The ability to change is a skill that requires intention, motivation, and preparation. Change sometimes involves stepping away from people and situations that may impede our success. We may start off with a life invested in lying, cheating, and stealing and realize there is a limited future in this way of being. Or, we may have been taught that it is acceptable to "just get by," doing the minimum amount of work required.

The motivation to change may occur out of desire or out of necessity. We may be on a path and willing to stumble along because there is a greater need and investment to keep things the same. Until a crisis occurs—which forces us to look at ourselves more deeply—change may appear unnecessary. However, crisis itself becomes the catalyst for change. Perhaps someone in our family dies, our spouse announces that the marriage is not working, or a child graduates from college and is ready to leave home. These stressful life events can occur at any time, but not everyone is ready to embrace change.

Before you accept or reject these possibilities, it may take someone outside of you, someone who believes in you and who's willing to be honest and open with you, for you to even consider the need for change. This person may be willing to provide feedback about parts of you that even you do not see in yourself. This most charitable human being may be telling you things you don't want to hear. They may do so at great risk, knowing that it may be the end of a relationship. Actually, the delivery of feedback is vital. It was noted by Kevin Ochsner, a psychology professor at Columbia University, that only 30 percent of feedback given is ever applied.[6] The receiver may be uncomfortable with the information and also feel unsafe about it being known and revealed.

Therefore, feedback must arrive in a safe environment with the words carefully selected to be sure the receiver is ready and able. It may then take great courage on your part, the receiver, to consider what is being said. Facing feedback that you may not agree with or that is so new to you that you can hardly believe what is being said, takes incredible resolve as you try to see things from a new perspective.

Chapter 1: The Building of Self

Exercising Choice

Each of us has a remarkable ability to exercise choice. To do so, we need to understand who we are, what we believe in, and the impact we have on others. Once again, this is a great reason to foster self-awareness. You owe this to yourself. It is my guess that, if you struggle with these concepts and are not open to feedback, the consequences will follow you in all parts of your life. If you fail to define yourself, be accountable, responsible, and dependable to your virtues and your values, how is it possible to expect others to trust you and remain loyal?

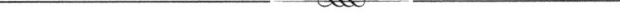

We have a remarkable ability to exercise choice. To do so we need to understand who we are, what we believe in, and the impact we have on others.

One beauty of life is that no two people are the same. Each of us starts out as a unique individual and open to opportunities to discover, enjoy, and honor the gifts born to us.

We are also influenced by a hierarchy of needs, especially the experience of safety and security. Maslow's inspiring 1943 paper, *A Theory of Human Motivation*,[7] indicates that needs are a clear motivating factor, with an ultimate goal of being the best we can possibly be. Maslow suggests that the first four levels of his hierarchy are Deficiency Needs, which are required for ultimate growth, followed by the Being Needs, occurring in self-actualization and self-fulfillment. His theory remains especially important to those directing clients to higher levels of comfort as Maslow indicates the importance in meeting Physiological, Safety, Belongingness, and Esteem Needs before the individual can ever hope to be at the pinnacle of self-fulfillment. Clearly, if you find yourself without a home, adequate food, or dealing with an abundance of fear and doubt, it is highly unlikely to be able to claim that you are "living your best life." This is the time to acknowledge that you may have some personal, and perhaps, interpersonal work to do.

An important goal for all humans is to address our past and correct experiences that may serve as obstacles to our personal and interpersonal goals. Drawing on his theory of interpersonal psychoanalysis, Harry Stack Sullivan addresses the source of difficulties we adopt during early development that contributes to the acceptance of *self* and the ability to develop relationships. Sullivan infers that loneliness is the most painful of all human experiences and that many of our efforts are designed to reduce the potential of being alone. Through interpersonal relationships, all behavior is directed toward getting needs met and reducing anxiety, all of which contributes to the shaping of our personality.[8]

Sullivan suggests that our caregivers have an incredible opportunity to foster messages that can lay the foundation for the developing psyche. The most worrisome message is when a child is ignored and actually left alone with a sense of total social isolation. The concepts outlined by Sullivan include thoughts that he coins as *Good Me, Bad Me,* and *Not Me.*

Could this inadequacy and social isolation contribute to the phenomenon when a child enters his school with a rifle, not worrying about consequences, yet wanting to be seen and heard?

We have learned over time that the episodes of mass violence seem to meet some distorted need to be seen. We also know that some adolescents and adults who are grieving are vulnerable and may make poor choices. There is evidence that they struggle with simple functions and well-established skills related to judgement. In their mind, they hear, "I no longer matter." Behavior exhibited may include going on dates that are unsafe. They may exercise promiscuity or ignore warnings about health risks like smoking and vaping. When a person lacks support and feedback, they struggle to achieve a sense of self-esteem and belonging, all of which impacts their decisions and actions.[9]

You may recognize the Maslow Pyramid and dismiss this as unimportant to you today. I suggest you take a closer look, as I did. I purposely weaved in the wisdom provided by a number of theorists to enrich your knowledge related to your early beginning and the development of *self*. In this case, Maslow recognized that life does not always play fair and that some of us have been granted a step up in the process toward achievement. Others may still be living paycheck to paycheck, hoping to have money to pay rent or buy food. Either you have been born with a golden spoon or are deprived and sitting at a lower level of the Maslow Pyramid. The obvious concern is how to use this knowledge to change your path.

Maslow became an important figure both within and outside of psychology. His work represents a movement in the direction of Humanistic Psychology where it is recognized that our greatest achievements rest in the ability to gain competence in *self* and move on to achieving successful interpersonal relationships. His theory has been under much scrutiny as there are some who are not convinced that the motivation of humans follows a hierarchy. However, even Maslow acknowledged that there is a possibility for some, given our uniqueness, to be more inclined to seek the need for self-esteem before the need for love. The great gift Maslow did provide is a simplistic approach in providing order and structure, whereby we can aspire to a greater sense of satisfaction and accomplishment.

A View of Abraham Maslow's Hierarchy of Needs Theory

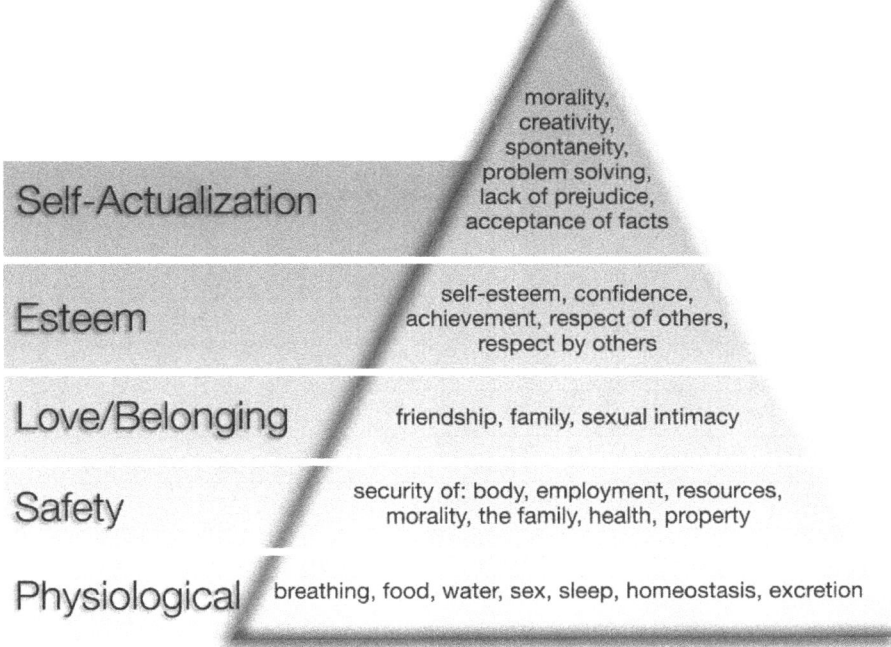

To help you determine your own sense of *self*, the exercises on the following pages provide some characteristics of individual achievements at each step of Maslow's Pyramid. It is important at this juncture to take every opportunity to better appreciate yourself.

Take a look at the list of characteristics. Where are you in Maslow's scheme of things? Have you noticed an ability to reach a higher level of competence at another time of your life and now seem to have slipped into a different level of success in meeting your needs? What are the circumstances that are contributing to this change?

Maslow's theory implies that people can move in and out of certain levels of the hierarchy depending on the "here and now" circumstances life presents. If, suddenly, a person loses their job and has no means of support or an ability to pay the rent, it is possible that the Safety and Security and Physiological Needs are at risk and no longer being met. One would expect that this individual would find difficulty in reaching Self-Actualization when needing to address lower level Being Needs. Meanwhile, you and others may now be considering you as "needy" because you can no longer accomplish what you had previously been successful at doing.

Exercise I: Identification of needs

The hierarchy of needs pyramid allows you to assess your present state and better understand what may be missing in your life. While the goal is to reach a place where you are the best you can be, you may have needs that have not yet been accomplished. For example, you may be seeking a sense of safety and security with a regular income, yet you are currently unemployed.

Using the lists below, look for examples that help you define your current state and take the time to write down your achievements. This allows you to define future goals and to tell your story.

_____
_____
_____
_____
_____
_____
_____
_____
_____
_____
_____
_____
_____
_____
_____
_____
_____
_____

Self-Actualization/Self-Fulfillment Needs

- Exhibit confidence and a willingness to take risks
- Comfortable in promoting others and their abilities
- Motivated by a strong sense of ethics
- Exhibit behavior that is autonomous, exhibiting independent thinking, not needing the comfort, approval, and security of always following the group

- Enjoy the experience of being alone
- Act spontaneously
- Understand process is as important as outcome
- Demonstrate morality, creativity, and problem-solving

Esteem Needs

- Gain the respect and appreciation of others
- Accomplishing goals and enjoying the recognition/respect of these efforts
- Demonstrate confidence, self-esteem, and achievement

Love and Belonging/Social Needs

- Ability to establish sustained friendships
- Becoming interested in romantic attachments, intimacy, and committed relationships, i.e., marriage
- Forming a family experience or establishing living arrangements that allow for social interactions
- Social groups at home or work
- Joining community groups, volunteering, and considering a cause, something in which we believe in
- Becoming a part of a religious organization

Physiological Needs

- Nutritious food to eat
- Safe water to drink
- Air to breathe
- Homeostasis i.e., temperature and shelter
- Sexual reproduction to participate in the propagation of the human species

Safety and Security Needs

- Financial security through the ability to find a job and maintain employment, manage resources, and property
- Achieving health and wellness, including the ability to obtain health insurance
- Contributing money to a savings account
- Safety against accidents and injury
- Moving, in order to live in an environment where one experiences greater safety

Exercise II: Who am I and who do I hope to be?

With an enhanced desire to achieve a sense of well-being by reaching a better understanding of *self*, it is important to have an awareness of engaging qualities you admire in yourself and later, those to whom you feel an attraction.

From the list below, select the top five engaging qualities that best describe you, the reason for the selection, and the meaning each has to you. Are there other engaging qualities on this list, or others that come to mind?

Engaging Qualities

able	helpful	relaxed
accepting	honest	religious
adaptable	idealistic	respected
aware	independent	responsive
bold	ingenious	searching
brave	intelligent	self-assertive
calm	introverted	self-assured
caring	kind	self-conscious
cheerful	knowledgeable	sensible
clever	logical	sentimental
complex	loving	shy
confident	mature	spontaneous
dependable	modest	sports-minded
dignified	nervous	sympathetic
empathetic	observant	tense
energetic	organized	trustworthy
extroverted	patient	warm
friendly	powerful	well-mannered
giving	proud	wise
happy	quiet	witty
	reflective	

Now add three additional engaging qualities worthy of your consideration. What made you choose these?

_____
_____
_____
_____

Exercise III: Reminders of life's character-shaping events

None of us are immune to situations or events in life that cause turmoil, hardship, and grief. Before you pack this chapter away and move on to the next, carefully review the list below. It is intended to remind you of life experiences that may contribute to your building of *self*. Some of these instances are examples of how you persevered and maybe even learned a few important lessons, while others may have left a permanent mark that easily raises feelings of sadness, joy, anger, or fear.

Your list could help you as you uncover and gain insight. Create your own list and any information you wish to share about these life events.[10]

- All the losses, illnesses, and major injuries that have occurred in your life and significant others' lives. Include any personal experiences where you faced your own potential death.
- Any disruptions you have experienced in your professional or work life, including the loss of a job, or a choice to leave a job.
- Any events that have impacted your safety and security, such as, the Holocaust, 9/11, the building of the wall along the southern border of the United States, or any other legal restrictions.
- Any difficult choices that have created a challenge or loss.
- Any difficulties in your romantic/personal life including the break-up of a cherished relationship, death of a spouse, the experience of living in an empty nest, or divorce.
- Any trauma experienced by moving to a new location including the circumstances around the move and your participation in decision-making.
- Any important losses of people, jobs, lifestyle, or dreams.
- Any disenfranchised loss, one in which a social indicator did not permit you to grieve openly, such as, a pet, ex-husband and his/her family, or a former supervisor with whom you had conflict.

The chapter on "The Building of Self" provides the underlying background of information to base your understanding of *self*. It also promotes your taking an active part in your self-discovery as you read this book. Yes, it will be your responsibility to consider any changes needed to support your desire for personal growth; no one else can do this work for you. Your effort will serve as a foundation as you continue on to build further awareness in the next chapters in this book. All that follows is preparing you to grieve your losses, accept your condition, change what needs to be changed, and find your joy again.

Remember that what you put into this process is what you will get out. If you can embrace the need to understand who you are, you will realize that you are an exceptional individual unlike anyone else you have ever met. At the same time, you will find that it is possible to be similar and have shared thoughts and needs with many others in this world. This is accomplishing "both/and."

This "both/and" concept, when used through life, allows you to accept many things that were not previously understood. In this case you can be both a unique creation who looks, thinks, feels, and acts like no other and also a human being with thoughts, feelings, and needs that align with the inner space of others.

My goal is for you to find yourself in the pages of this book. It is time to gain insight and accept who you want to be. I am encouraging you to first look within yourself. That is where you will find the person that has supported you throughout your life. It is for you to determine whether you need to reframe your engaging qualities. Use this as a chance to grow, to accept, and to forgive—all in an effort to better understand how to reach a sense of peace and wholeness. This is where you will find that strength within.

It is such a pleasure for me to work with you on the basics of the human condition, in being in tune with yourself and others.

2

There's a Place for Us

Be sure to congratulate yourself on the work you completed in Chapter 1. If you read it thinking it wasn't worthy of your time or wouldn't be meaningful to you, think again and choose wisely. After all, we're talking about your happiness here. Developing you and your personal *self* takes work and is a precursor to the success of any relationship you choose to engage in throughout your life. Each of us is accountable for our own happiness. While some still wait for the day when that prince or princess will magically arrive, the wait may be a long one. It's more likely that you will find that person when you have done the work necessary to find *you*, and hopefully in the end, become your biggest fan.

When we gaze inside ourselves and become honest with what we find there, it is called introspection. It means taking a good long look at every part of the "you" you have become, including things like your appearance and the first impression you make on others—either in person or online. Your engaging characteristics are reflected in your actions, your beliefs, and the messages you send out to the world (e.g., on social media). The people you currently attract and the ones you wish you could add to your social circle are influenced by their perceptions of you.

Perceptions are powerful aspects of who we are as people. These include sensory information of sight, taste, and smell influenced by what is seen and heard. The information is then carried to the brain and combined with knowledge, judgement, and experience. Perceptions can also be impacted by a person's beliefs and values, even biases and preconceived prejudices. All this then combines to result in an impression. That impression may be the thing that makes or breaks the opportunity to continue to relate in a personal way, or even be invited back for a second encounter. F. Scott Fitzgerald tells us, "It's never too late to be whoever you want to be…I hope you live a life you are proud of, and if you find that you are not, I hope you have the strength to start over."

While we may have little control over a person's previous experience, we have a responsibility to know who we are, what we believe and value, and how we proceed to share this information.

"It's never too late to be whoever you want to be…I hope you live a life you are proud of, and if you find that you are not, I hope you have the strength to start over."

—*F. Scott Fitzgerald*

Starting over may be the price you have to pay for having lived in your comfort zone, the emotional spot that you believe provides comfort and security and where you maintain the status quo at all cost. However, some live in this place beyond the time it serves as a place of comfort and security. Maintaining the same beliefs and responses over and over can actually inhibit growth in ourselves and those around us. While looking at things objectively, it's an important practice to keep yourself in check and aligned with ever-changing norms. Consider the tone of your verbal, written, and non-verbal expressions. These all serve as a window to your feelings—especially those showing signs of love, frustration, anger, fear, anxiety, and disgust. Allow yourself the opportunity to demonstrate who you truly are—the whole of you—including your thoughts and feelings. If you find that you have been having difficulty forming (and keeping) relationships, an honest evaluation and assessment of yourself may be the best next step.

Psychologists have maintained interest in concepts related to an individual's awareness of *self*. For example, any one of us may be convinced that we are clear in our communication, while in fact, we may be masking our true *self*. The work presented in 1955 by Joseph Luft and Harry Ingham, in their creation of the Johari Window, provides evidence that there are four parts of the human experience that manifest in a relationship.[11]

The Johari Window

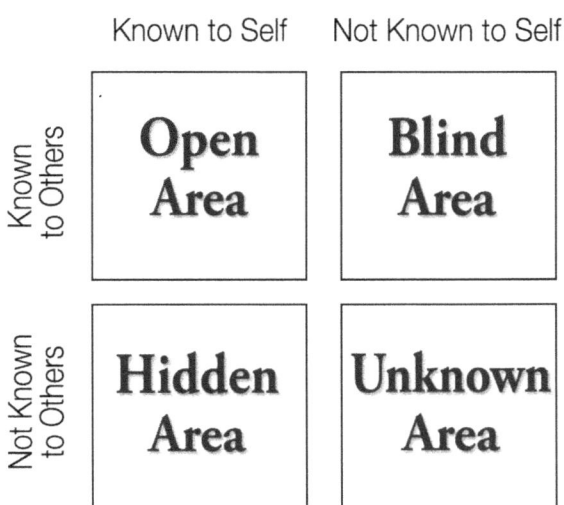

You may ask how it is even possible to be unaware of your own characteristics or idiosyncrasies while proceeding through life. You may genuinely believe that you are in touch with yourself and honest and open to others. In truth, there are times others *do* know you better than you know yourself, especially in areas where you have been closed off and self-protective when trying to avoid displaying your true feelings.

My own sons tell a story about our day trip into New York City when they were young. Recalling the "Unknown Area" described in the Johari Window as deeper aspects of one's personality, I was not aware of the extent of my feelings and behaviors which arose in response to danger and a need to protect. While waiting for the bus back to New Jersey, my son, Michael, who was then eight, was approached by a man who took an interest in a souvenir he was holding. I perceived this man as a threat as he moved too close to Michael's personal space and had his hand on his shoulder. This was a time when many of us were aware that child snatching was a reality. While usually mild-mannered, I immediately took action, responding the way a mother lion protects her cubs. I reacted loudly by telling the man to step away and behaviorally by taking hold of my son. While too young to understand the potential danger, the boys responded with considerable surprise, thinking their mother had lost it. However, they learned the lesson of standing up for oneself, which was a hard one as it compromised the sense of safety they hoped to achieve through avoidance.

Consider your own experiences to add to your understanding of the Johari Window. As noted in Chapter 1, some of us were taught that the role of a child was to "be seen and not heard." Others were encouraged to find their voice and state their position openly. It is possible to support that child within you and still manage relationships and situations by being true to yourself and expressing yourself openly while, at the same time, being mindful of the opportunity to win others over.

Open Area
Allows for Individuals to have the greatest exchange of information free from distractions, mistrust, confusion, conflict and misunderstandings.

Blind Area
Is often referred to as that part of ourselves where we lack or avoid awareness of self. The aim in every individual and relationship is to reduce this area and increase the open area in order to increase self-awareness.

Hidden Area
This is what is known to ourselves and unknown to others. It includes anything you know about yourself, but that is kept from others and typically represents deep dark secrets or simply information you fear may influence the way others view you. It can also include hidden agendas or manipulative plans. Reducing the hidden area improves open communication and improved relationships.

Unknown Area
This contains feelings, information and experiences unknown to both the person and others. It can represent feelings, behaviors, attitudes, and aptitudes, which can be quite close to the surface, and which can be positive and useful; or they can be deeper aspects of a person's personality, influencing his/her behavior to various degrees. Large unknown areas would typically be expected in younger people, and people who lack experience or self-belief.

Chapter 2: There's a Place for Us

The application of the Johari Window encourages individuals to make the Open Area as active as possible while reducing the size of the other areas. This is done by regular and honest exchange of feedback and a willingness to disclose personal feelings. People around you will understand what "makes you tick," and what you find easy or difficult to do and can provide appropriate support. And of course, you can then do the same for them.

The Johari Window helps people better understand their interpersonal communication and relationships. It encourages us to become conscious of all parts of our personal being. It especially promotes wholeness within areas where we may be blinded yet are still sending out messages for the world to see and react to. I encourage you to select someone from your inner circle—your social atom—who can provide you with feedback about how you are perceived in a variety of situations.

To be successful in this task requires an element of trust and openness along with a willingness to hear the good, the bad, and the ugly. Ideally, you may want to welcome someone into your perimeter who is willing to be honest and to maintain confidentiality as they provide concrete examples to help you grow and learn about yourself. For example, you may be interested in knowing whether you gain respect for your ideas based upon the validity of your statements or whether people listen to you based upon the clarity and delivery of your thoughts and feelings. Or, do people tend to shy away because you project an air of arrogance, confusion, or indecisiveness and that you lack a willingness to support others' views?

Most people believe they are listened to because of the value of their ideas. However, there may be a desire to align with you, not only based on what you say, but also due to the perception of integrity in all you do. This trust is earned and may take time and effort to demonstrate. When you speak, others are paying attention to the words you use, the expressions you select, your posture, and your attitude.

As you proceed through your journey of change you will notice that you have the power to develop relationships that make the best use of the person you have become. Keep this phrase in mind, "What you send out, you get back." If you approach people with kindness and warmth, you generally receive a smile and a kind word in response. If you walk into a situation appearing preoccupied by thoughts about previous events or are rehearsing and planning your responses to something that is raising your anxiety, you may receive an abrupt and disarming reaction. It is for you to decide how you want to be treated and remembered.

It's ironic how we sometimes believe we're invisible and that our behavior is insignificant to others. Well, guess again! All behavior has meaning, and a simple effort allows us to demonstrate meaningful behavior that represents the person we want others to know.

I learned an important lesson from a hospital CEO when I worked at a medical system in Western North Carolina. I share this story when I teach others about their own significance; it serves as an important reminder to those of us who want another chance and another opportunity to gain love and respect from the world around us.

Each week I attended a large required business meeting with the hospital directors. We were not the biggest "gorilla" in the health care arena in this region and recognized the importance of maintaining market share to be sure we were economically solvent. John, the CEO, regularly reminded us that being perceived as offering excellence in service to our patients and the community required not only meeting and exceeding quality metrics, but also demonstrating consistently professional behavior.

John began each meeting with this reminder, "When you are walking along Main Street, waiting for a parking space or a dinner reservation, when you are at church or in your favorite supermarket, *remember, people are watching and they are watching all of the time.* Be sure to represent us well in all of these circumstances." At first, I thought John was being a bit paranoid, but I soon realized the value of his statement. You only have one chance to make a *first* impression and it may become a lasting one.

Becoming clear about who you are and what you believe will serve as a strong influence in how people see you and who you attract. You have complete control over the ability to gather like-minded people. Liking yourself and being true to yourself is a crucial factor in developing relationships that can ride the storms and position you to experience the joy of living.

Equally as important is recognizing that the days of believing you are incomplete without another person to fill your life and make you whole are over. Years ago, I had the privilege of hearing Dr. Bernie Siegel speak at a conference on healing. A renowned pediatric surgeon working primarily with cancer survivors, Dr. Siegel captured my heart when he declared, "Each of us comes into this world perfectly imperfect." For me, his words of wisdom serve as a reminder that we are who we need to be upon arrival. While we may stumble and fall along the way, we have the ability to grow and change to improve the conditions that may keep us from achieving personal greatness and fulfillment.

Whether you are an advocate of a principle that inspires individual enlightenment as a path to wholeness or you support psychologists like Carl Jung, who encourage us to appreciate knowledge from within our unconscious, or if you have led a life seeking your truth from a faith rich in Judeo-Christian beliefs, the outcome is much the same. As we proceed from birth to death, we travel in a unidirectional path where humans are offered opportunities to learn, to assimilate information, and to adapt. The work we do to define ourselves provides a greater opportunity to love ourselves.

Chapter 2: There's a Place for Us

Define yourself, love and appreciate yourself, and you will easily attract others into your life. We are constantly encouraged to reach clarity in our beliefs and to aspire to a life of wholeness in thought, mind, and spirit. As discussed in Chapter 1, developmental psychologists call this *individuation*. This then becomes the foundation of your identity.

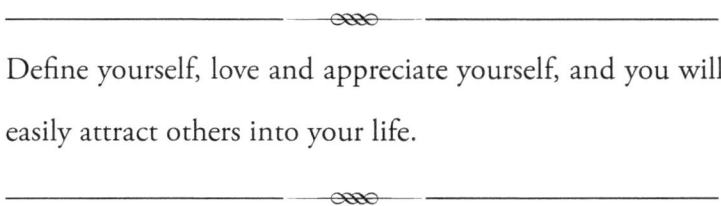

Define yourself, love and appreciate yourself, and you will easily attract others into your life.

Reaching this place requires time and energy to be devoted not only to maintaining the person you have become, but to directing your attention outwardly to others through 1:1 relationships, or by becoming an active, contributing member of a sound and productive family, a valuable organization, a committed community, and a dynamic society. In fact, you may know someone in your life who has reached a sense of comfort in knowing their personal worth and now seeks out opportunities to promote the talents of others.

I immediately think of Bill and Melinda Gates, who are known for advancing scholarship and have contributed considerable effort and financial support for global health issues, including prevention strategies, providing vaccines, and other tangible treatment for diseases. Let me be quite clear: This is not about money, but more about your willingness to invest yourself in something for someone. Take into account the acts of kindness you may have done: How would you like to be remembered?

As a society, it is not only desirable, but necessary to encourage others to reach their potential. In the event you are a person who finds yourself asking, "What's in it for me?," consider that the joy derived from helping others reach a place of fulfillment can sometimes be more rewarding than achieving this for yourself. People too easily talk themselves out of participating in anything. They are convinced they are inadequate or their contribution will not be enough to matter. Start with one small thing and watch it grow until your passion takes over. Take responsibility for change. It is only then you can begin to take credit for the changes you add to make the world a better place.

In my work as a consultant, our lodging and meals were included as part of the daily expenses allocated for each project. Each night, our team met for dinner where food was often more than we needed. One evening, we realized that each of us was wasting an incredible amount that could easily support people in the community. While we did not want to encourage anyone taking to the streets, there already were camps of homeless people throughout the city. Putting away our fears of getting mugged or insulting others by our effort, we decided to venture out and ask folks if they would accept our food. This small token became a frequent event. Many of us began to purposely decrease our intake so that we had adequate food available to share. Our desire to help was well-received and served to supplement food for those who had so little. We continued to feel grateful for what we had, and most of all, our ability to make a difference.

Remember, the person you want to be is already in the making. The work you do to clarify your understanding of who you are serves as your blueprint. Strengthening the clarity and conviction about the qualities that are important to you will cause you to live by them. Whether at home, at work, or in seeking new relationships, you will find yourself selecting and enjoying the experience of others who fit into your framework. Specifically, if you send out love, love will come back to you. If you send out a message of being open, honest, independent, and capable, you will attract others who are much the same as you. Conversely, if you exhibit behaviors that indicate that you are needy and unsure of that which you believe, your life could be filled with individuals who are hoping to control, to direct, and perhaps to diminish you.

Too often, a relationship begins with one or both individuals lacking clarity and confidence in themselves and the person they hope to attract. Humans have a strong desire to be liked and accepted. When unsuccessful in filling our lives with loving, honest people, we may deny our standards and values and allow people in our lives who may not adequately meet our needs. They might fill a gap when loneliness becomes unbearable, but most of us want and need more.

Quite simply, most of us want to belong to something and someone and to create a life upon which we can depend. This could be the case when dating someone who is currently married to someone else. Their reality is that they may not be capable of committing to you. These relationships last for a while before one or both members recognize that trying to please and be someone they are not is virtually impossible. One of you will need to take that hard look, and with thoughtfulness, evaluate the merit in making this compromise.

First, know what you believe in and what you hope to experience in life, then be willing to stand by this truth. Anything less than truth and honesty places the relationship in jeopardy from the start. This process is fundamental to establishing a successful connection with others. The goal is to achieve a sense of satisfaction and comfort in yourself and then seek similar qualities in others as you proceed to make choices about your relationships. This translates into finding safety and security, self-esteem, and a sense of loving and belonging with people who have also made the effort to understand the same for themselves.

You and Others in Relationship

In researching the topic of relationships, the consistent message is that the most successful relationships—the ones that stand the test of time—are made up of people who have accepted and acknowledged that the only constant in life is change. They have a willingness to remain open to change and are often willing to adapt. We always hope that while we grow and change, people who matter to us will see the benefit and want to embrace our effort.

Social psychologists tell us that a change in one part of the system automatically creates a change in the entire system. The system in this case is a relationship or family. Therefore, while we are eager to begin to experience the joy of awareness and success, there is no guarantee that even the people who are most important in our lives are willing to consider what these changes mean to them or how they affect their willingness to return your relationship to equilibrium. As stated by the classical pianist Arthur Rubinstein, "Of course there is no formula for success except, perhaps, an unconditional acceptance of life and what it brings." It truly becomes important to recognize the concept that no man is an island. Therefore, our growth and resulting changes in behavior or attitude must include acknowledging the impact of our transformations on others.

"Of course, there is no formula for success except, perhaps, an unconditional acceptance of life and what it brings."
—*Arthur Rubinstein, classical pianist*

Surround Yourself with Loving People

A significant goal, then, is to surround yourselves with *loving people* who support your ability to flourish and who strengthen your personal best as you reciprocate to them. Loving people do not always agree with everything you do or hold as true. Rather, loving people remain genuine and authentic to you and to your relationship despite differences. At times they challenge us and our thinking. Yet, they exhibit a willingness to communicate their thoughts and their feelings to be better understood and to enable progress in the relationship.

If you find yourself in a relationship that stifles you, creates pain or fear, or becomes one-sided, it may be time to stop and review. Look back at your own guiding principles—the qualities, values, and beliefs that have become important to you—and determine whether the relationship in question still holds value. Once again, you may need to ask if either member has outgrown the relationship because you have learned more about yourself and the world you have created.

You do sometimes face the risk that your growth may not be keeping in step with the values, attitudes, and beliefs of the other person. This can happen to any of us. It creates a situation where we may ask whether we can remain content in this relationship. Or perhaps the other person can't or won't consider their own potential to develop. Maybe they're not willing to do the work it takes to remain in relationship with you. This may produce an "aha" moment that leads you to question whether you're willing to go to a place where you confront your own reality by challenging the relationship or let the awareness pass.

As children, it is ingrained in us to avoid danger at all cost. If you are currently aware of a problem in your relationship, it is likely that the issue has been occurring over time. Either you or the person you share the relationship with can communicate that the relationship is in trouble. But we often avoid "touching the hot stove," which means not acknowledging your true thoughts out of fear that the relationship will crumble toward its demise. Speaking our truth may in fact hurt. This experience can occur in friendships, close family ties, and may also occur in work relationships.

As I turn to the writings of my dear daughter-in-law, Jordan Parker Reed, I find that through her studies to become a yogi in New York City, she learned the important yogic practice of *Aparigraha* or non-attachment.[12] Jordan is a Millennial and has gained a different perspective for coping with loss and preparing for people to come and go due to the decisions they make in attempting to find a better life. For those of us who struggle with loss, it always feels like it's all about me. As a staunch disciple of attachment and belonging theory and having experienced the grave impact when feeling rejected, abandoned, or isolated, I find this ability to better understand the virtues of non-attachment quite curious.

The lesson brought me back to a time when I was 18 and in college. I was the first in my family to live in a dorm in a state far away from home. By the end of the first semester, as my father's health diminished, my parents sold our family home in New York and moved to Florida. I felt lost and unsure as the new location was not my home. In fact, I never returned to my parent's home. Instead of dwelling on a sense of abandonment, I realized it was time to figure out how to live on my own and I found myself exercising the process of non-attachment.

Through Jordan's experience as a credentialed yogi, she explains that *Aparigraha* translates to non-greed, non-possessiveness, or non-attachment. And others wiser than I have suggested, "Humans become attached to the feelings around what things or people give to us, not necessarily the objects or people themselves."[13] With these two schools of thought in mind, it's important to recognize that nothing is forever while fully cherishing the reason people come into our lives, even those relationships that may be controversial or short-lived. Sometimes, people come into our lives to validate us. At other times, people come to create just enough turmoil to initiate change, forcing us to see things from a different perspective.

This may be easier said than done. Therefore, most of us do experience a sense of loss and may need to find ways in which we can easily cope while not fully accepting or understanding the motives of others. It is particularly helpful to accept the perspective of others by engaging in a practice where we completely turn around our thinking and beliefs and work on seeing things from the other side or another person's reality. It may even require tracing back to the person's life and placing yourself in their shoes.

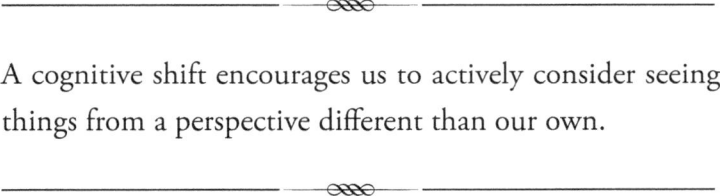

A cognitive shift encourages us to actively consider seeing things from a perspective different than our own.

Unlike other members of the animal kingdom, humans engage in multiple simultaneous relationships based on roles we play. These may hold a variety of significance. Some of these relationships may seem unimportant, yet as you become more in touch with yourself, it is reasonable that you will also become more selective so that your relationships fall into the distinguished class of *loving people*. Whether it's your favorite grocery store clerk, your physician, or your dry cleaner, think about the reception you receive and the feelings you have when you engage in a relationship with these folks. Since life presents us with many instances that are totally out of our control, how energizing it is to take charge of the things you can and to be certain that your life is filled with people who matter most to you.

So, if you need a hairdresser who is skilled and honest, select someone who can live up to this. And conversely, if someone or something gives you more grief than pleasure, consider how to change that picture or even how to let it go. The analogies are striking when we turn to important relationships in our lives. It is by our choice to remain in a relationship when the love has ended. It is also our choice to enter new relationships with a new set of eyes, with expectations or desires that match our newly found self.

The Differences Among Us

I recall the many required visits to the confessional booth during my years of growing up in the Catholic Church. It was there I was taught that I needed to be penitent and recite prayers for the *many* sins for which I needed to be forgiven. In truth, more times than not, I couldn't think of any sins I had committed. I found myself mentioning things like "speaking unkindly to my great aunt." It actually struck me that at times I was making up a sin, in effect telling a lie, in order to meet the expectation of the nun who marched us through this process each week. It wasn't until later in life that I realized this method of seeking forgiveness had become artificial and lacked meaning for me. More importantly, I realized that forgiveness was an essential value to me and my immediate family and that it was in my power to create change around the way in which I asked for it.

As a result, I began to question my faith tradition as a young adult. While I was certain about my relationship with God, I struggled with what I saw as man-made decisions that made it harder for me to live my life as a "good" Catholic. For example, I often wondered how accidentally eating a bologna sandwich on a Friday made me such a bad person that if I failed to go directly to confession, I might end up in hell should I die before receiving forgiveness from a priest. This seemed much more complicated and controlling for a discerning individual like me. After all, I was already filling my life with loving people and trying my best to be the same.

To provide an acceptable compromise before taking the even more radical action of choosing to observe a different faith, I decided I would only visit the confessional on days when a benevolent priest would be there to hear confessions. This was someone who actually listened to my concerns about life and how I may have strayed. He would even sometimes laugh with me when he recognized that my "sins" were really just my feeble attempts to negotiate with the world. So, even though I had been indoctrinated to accept what was put before me as a given part of my faith, I learned there were both loving and not-so-loving people representing my God. The loving priests recognized we all make mistakes and had the ability to coach me to do better; the not-so-loving priests were still making their decisions out of their traditional beliefs without the awareness of the need to compromise.

This reality was also validated at an even younger age when the nun who taught my catechism class told me that there was "no place in heaven for my father." In the Catholic faith, going to heaven was and is very significant. And to a faithful child, it's a basic cornerstone of living a life of kindness to others. However, the nun was very clear that because my father was Jewish, "he would perish forever." I'm happy to report that even then I had the *chutzpah* that my father, the "Jewish man," had taught me. I marched my six-year-old self, crying all the way, to our parish priest who assured me that he knew the kind deeds of my father and went on to tell me that God would find him a place in heaven.

When we feel hurt, challenged, or misunderstood, we typically become defensive and need to prove that we are right. Have you ever experienced the situation where you find yourself participating in an argument only to realize that you had won the battle, but lost the war?

For instance, during boardroom arguments, a point of view often emerges to settle a difference. Despite the semblance of order and agreement, the person opposing the intended outcome is viewed as a renegade that needs to be controlled. At what cost did the person win the argument, only to find themselves losing other advantages that may later affect their job security?

Sitting in couple sessions, I have had my share of being a mediator to two people who started out loving each other and vowing to remain together under a variety of circumstances. In my bold and often paradoxical approach, I would often ask what happened to those promises. Despite whatever challenges life presents us, the point of being in relationship with others is to connect. If it takes a special effort to be kind and respectful, so be it, as it takes a commitment on the part of all in a relationship to be willing to grow as a unit and to learn how to navigate differences.

It is never about winning an argument at the expense of another, and if that's the case, it's merely ego standing in the way of a quality relationship. There are times when we have to ask ourselves if it is better to give in and accept the perspective of the other person or do we need to defend our ego and insist on having things our way? This could be as simple as, "You selected the restaurant the last time, so I get to choose," or "I remember agreeing to pay off the house before we start searching for a new one."

Most of the time, people will make decisions and insist on the outcome they choose based upon their feelings, opinions, and beliefs. Often, people either avoid or neglect explaining the value and importance they place on these decisions. This leaves a partner at a clear disadvantage. Until such time as we learn to value ourselves, our relationships, and others, we may fail to see that there is an abundance of possible consequences each time we speak or act. Be prepared with as much accountability as possible as you manage to reach success with each relationship. In doing so, we also need to take responsibility for the role we play in the outcome—the good, the bad, and the ugly. This give and take is called compromise.

At a deeper level, when feeling challenged, it is vital that you know what the "it" is that's disturbing you about the situation or the communication. How important is the "it" to the bigger scheme of life that you are willing to verbalize the concern and perhaps risk the relationship? Is this the sword upon which you choose to fall? Or, metaphorically, are you willing to risk killing the relationship? You will feel the sense of comfort and accomplishment when you realize and embrace the qualities that define you.

By reaching a better understanding of *self*, you start to establish boundaries. These boundaries will include all the engaging qualities, values, attitudes, and beliefs that you see as important. You gain a better sense of those characteristics you consider as non-negotiable and those where you can accept deviations. This is the process of learning to appreciate the differences among us. This allows us to honor ourselves while also co-existing with an individual or individuals who see things differently.

However, once you have defined and prioritized that which is most important to you in life, it is your responsibility to put this into words in a conversation with the people who are meaningful to you. For example, if you expect your significant other to be faithful, they need to know this is a priority. Relationships take work, constant revision, and sometimes renegotiation of the rules as your needs and those of your partner's change or become clearer.

Remember the earlier statement that says, "What you send out, you get back." This is based on a biblical passage that reminds us to, "Be not deceived; God is not mocked: For whatsoever a man soweth, that shall he also reap."[14] This boils down to: If you send out love and kindness, there is a greater opportunity to experience love. It is also possible to stimulate the very worst in people when we send out messages that create fear or judgement. Feelings of fear and anxiety are contagious, often promoting the same in others. Some go so far as to say that the things that we judge in others may also be the parts of ourselves that we dislike. Are you frightened or feeling vulnerable? Do you detect anger or anxiety in yourself or others?

When you are in a personal state of uncertainty, it is acceptable to wait to be fully ready to engage. Before you risk "touching the hot stove," take the time to get clear about what you hope to accomplish. It is always wise to ask yourself, "What do I need?" When interacting with people who are immature in their psychological or social development, conversation may not be a welcomed intervention. Also, remember that no matter how hard you may try, some people simply don't fit with who you are becoming.

The person you are striving to become has a better understanding of themselves. You will do the work it takes to embrace your early beginning and accept the influences you experience along the way. You are hoping to understand everything in your life which may have had an effect on you becoming the person you are today. You are doing this work to accept your past and carve out a future that better prepares you to cope with all the life lessons that may come your way. The ultimate goal is to fully accept yourself for who you are, repair any bumps and blemishes, and find a path to fit in so that you can fill your life with loving people.

3

We Are Family

Take a moment and visualize the people around you in your life—those who represent your beginning, as well as parts of your past and present. These are the people we call family.

They create a rich legacy as they hold knowledge of our history. Some even lived the same experiences and shared family traditions that contributed to our beginning and the creation of our *self*. Family members provide us with a sense of belonging, acceptance, and comfort as we often carry similar traits and qualities that justify exactly who we are. They give us hope for survival by passing down stories of courageous and resolute ancestors who have worked to provide us with a better life. Regardless, family holds profound meaning: It contributes to the development of values, attitudes, beliefs, and opinions held by each individual.

Family can also shape the person you become by providing expectations about relationships and community that were likely established generations before you were born. Plans for your life, including the work you might do or the people you may seek, may have been in play well before you were born, when your parents entertained their dream about who you would become. Denying the whole or any part of these influences represents a loss.

With this hold so powerful, it's no surprise that most therapy sessions and even casual conversations about our life and personal growth centers around family. Historically, Freudian therapists tended to hold family responsible for why individuals experienced the conflicts that they carried on into adult life. It was especially believed that our mothers were the source of most of our controversies. In an effort to heal, individuals were often encouraged to have frequent therapy sessions to divulge the "truth" about their early beginnings, even at times resolving this history by confronting family members.

The Gestalt therapist side of me encourages you to acknowledge all of your parts—both past and present—and seek awareness of your thoughts and feelings to carefully reintroduce the knowledge and wisdom your past may provide you. Historical accounts allow you a richer understanding into your personal development.

Go ahead and ask your family members about their experiences in life. Encourage them to help you become more aware of how they see you and what you represent to the family. Hopefully they will provide their perception and their version of the truth without redacting.

This activity is quite different from that of my Freudian forefathers. While most of the psychotherapies we know today began with Freud and his analytic approach, Fritz Perls and others have provided a way to challenge the individual in reaching wholeness through a joining of thoughts and feelings.

Gestalt therapists encourage you to understand the influence your past may have on who you are today. This is important work to do. It is essential to understand that the intent is not about uncovering information aimed at blaming or shaming others. It is encouraging you to acknowledge every situation that may influence a perception of your reality.

As children, our memory is skewed by an immature cognitive ability. Children also have quite limited command of language. Young children may not recall or understand important situations or events that shape a family although they may vaguely remember the tone of communication.

It is possible that a child will remember a feeling or an emotion attached to that time. Because they lack a filter to determine "what is mine and what is yours," children often blame themselves for whatever is occurring in their environment. Interestingly they take on the responsibility of things they perceive they caused or to which they contributed based on their behavior. If parents are arguing, children naturally assume it was because they were creating a problem in the environment. It goes directly back to the worry of not being good enough.

As an adult, you have a choice in accepting messages from your past and learning from them or letting them take hold and consume you. At this point in your life, you have learned to take in information and discriminate what part of the occurrence is yours. And, you also have the ability to clarify concerns. Taking the time to include your family members in your process is more about reaching a new understanding or validating what you believe happened in your life. You can use this information to improve your awareness of missing pieces of family history and better understand the behaviors and choices made by others that may have impacted your life.

With the ability to think as an adult, you may be able to draw new conclusions that may even comfort you. If you learn a different interpretation of your past from different family members, consider yourself lucky—this gives more "grist for the mill" as the additional information will help guide you and your understanding.

Exploring your past is a significant step in reaching a better understanding of your life before you had clarity about your thoughts and feelings. This effort is not about uncovering information that will serve to blame and shame others. It is meant to provide more information about the choices and decisions that were made for you before you had a voice.

How you ask for this information, and what you do with it, is particularly important. If you are looking for a reason to disown your family and move on, you will likely send that message across when interviewing family members. If your intention is to heal, there is value in gathering all of the facts. I once knew a young man whose parents divorced when he was a teenager. With an incredible amount of validation from the maternal side of his family, the young man chose to blame his father and then legally disown him and his entire family by changing his last name to his mother's maiden name. The loss was more than he realized; it created many broken hearts that could not be repaired.

While it is important to acknowledge that both the husband and the wife make or break a marital relationship, families often choose to pick sides and blame one of the parties. In this case, at his young age, he was unable to discriminate and took on his mother's story and made it his reality.

It is true that many of your characteristic parts, including your attitudes, opinions, values, and beliefs, have been inherited from your family of origin or based on influences from life experiences with teachers, clergy, peers, colleagues, or important world events. Once again, children listen to what is being said and interpret it based on their cognitive ability or thinking skills at their stage of development. The proficiency and sophistication around the ability to fully comprehend happens over time and not at a precise date since each of us develops at our own pace.

Before the twentieth century, children were believed to be miniature adults having the same abilities as the adults in their environment. With intentionally designed models of education and psychology, Jean Piaget created an entire school of cognitive development and spent considerable time observing children from their stage of infancy. His own children were well-known to be part of his laboratory. His effort concluded that children operate on several processes of learning, in the manner in which they adapt and assimilate new information. He was convinced that introducing complex ideas needed to come at a time when the child could accept the knowledge being provided.

We now know through Piaget and his successors, that children think differently and are learning all of the time.[15] Each child goes through stages in the same order, yet child development is determined by biological maturation and interaction with the environment. Therefore, children in the same family may have different experiences of critical events.

Being the mother of two sons born 11 months apart quickly taught me that each human being is born with certain attributes, interests, and styles that set each apart as unique. Their environment was basically the same and therefore, a constant. Yet, they progressed at different levels of speech, mobility, and willingness to learn. They each had different curiosities, yet the one clear attribute they had in common was the powerful bond they built between them, a bond unlike any other relationship they experienced in their young lives. They felt entirely safe as long as they could be in each other's sight.

By one or two years of age, children are generally able to understand and respond to words, identify objects, and tell the difference in the people around them. However, they have difficulty filtering out what is theirs and what may be a condition that impacts the family socially, financially, emotionally, and spiritually. In keeping with an effort to enlighten, all of this work is important in understanding ways in which you may have developed your own level of intelligence, as well as the origins of your ability to adapt and accept new ways of being. Children have a distinct disadvantage at seeing things from a different perspective, while adults have the capacity to learn new ways to view the same event. The skill involved at seeing things from many sides is a learned response and a valuable one when considering the many times we disagree about real life situations that are before us. There is skill required to turn the situation around so that you are taking the position of the other person long enough to experience their position. This is known as a cognitive shift and is especially important as you investigate further into your family of origin and find any differences in opinion and memory from a variety of family members.

The concept of family is powerful during the early stages of our identity. For most of us, it represents our belonging and acceptance. For some, family explains it all: Your traditions, your food, your ethics, your choices. Family can influence your future when you follow expected and long-established beliefs. Your professional or work-related ties possibly were someone else's unfulfilled model for success. This is demonstrated when you hear the old adage that every family needs a "doctor, lawyer, or Indian chief." This can be a source of great disappointment when the young adult fails to achieve the family's expectations.

Be especially mindful of the instinct to rush back to your family to blame them for the actions and behaviors exhibited in their younger days. I am a firm believer that most of us make the very best choices we can with the knowledge and emotional conscience we have. Why would we *not* choose the best option?

More times than not, people mess up without intending to bring harm to others, but because they either don't see any other option or simply don't know better.

In a similar manner, if you find yourself in a relationship involving the addition of a whole new family, remember to appreciate the conditions that come with this occurrence. No two families are alike. Yet, when we fall in love and want to be included, it can be a difficult passage, as we often unconsciously hope to find all the characteristics we admired in our family of origin while finally being free of all we disliked.

Generations

If you recall, Developmental Theory recognizes the many tasks that occur as we age. During their time of "individuation and separation," adolescents may step away from their family's values and align with other adults or members of their peer group. Such a disruption can be the result of long-term illness, the death of a parent, divorce, or unemployment leading to financial insecurity. Much research is being done on the psychological and developmental characteristics of individuals, starting with Baby Boomers, Gen X, Millennials, Gen Z or the "pivotal" generation, and the emerging Alpha Generations.
Reading about and understanding the differences in these generations can only enhance our ability to successfully relate to them. Let's break them down:

- Baby Boomers were born in the era between 1946-64. This was the group that developed traits of greater individualism. With the threat of a draft to the Vietnam War, Boomers took on the world with rebellion, protests, and a desire for greater independence.

- Gen Xers, born during the 1960s to the early 1980s, were children emerging during a time of shifting societal values. Generally known as "latchkey children," this group often had both parents employed outside of the home to maintain financial security. Adult supervision was transferred to sitters or day care. A result is that members of Generation X tend to support a greater work-life balance, a desire to have fun (even at work), technological advancements, flexibility, and self-sufficiency.

- Millennials, born from 1981-1996, are best known to be adventurous. They have an entrepreneurial spirit, which is demonstrated in their willingness to change jobs, all based on an ideology to attain a better life. They have been criticized for their lack of loyalty; however, they lived through times in which corporations just as easily separated their parents and them from employment. They learned that years of service did not offer a "gold watch" at retirement and more readily created insecurity around ageism. Millennials also faced the uncertainties of massive terrorism in 9/11 and high school shootings, such as Columbine, Sandy Hook, and Stoneman Douglas.

- Pivotals, also known as Gen Z, represent the population born from 1995-2012. They are a generation facing and demanding greater equality as a given, not an option. For example, they insist upon equal rights for members of the LGBTQ community and equal pay for women. While there are similarities to previous groups, there seems to be a pendulum swing. Gen Z demonstrates a style centered around personal success. As a result, their demands are viewed as having a more global influence. They also tend to be more inclusive and have a willingness to "put their money where their mouth is." They are known to have spurred consumerism, have lived through ISIS, the first African American president, and the political sequelae from the election of Donald Trump.

- Generation Alphas have birth dates starting in 2010 and ending in the mid-2020s, so the majority of this cohort are still toddlers, pre-teens, or have yet to be born. However, it is projected that this generation will reach a total of two billion people worldwide by the time the youngest are born in 2025. The Alphas are the children of the Millennials. Since a majority of Millennials were raised by both parents, they place parenthood and marriage far above career and financial success.[16] We have yet to see the influence of this and other values on this latest generation.

Chapter 3: We Are Family

Family Configuration Models

While the term family generally represents those individuals who live within a particular household, the definitions have changed over time to support contemporary lifestyles. In 2020, for the first time, The United States Census Bureau reflects a change in the structure of family to include: "opposite-sex husband/wife/spouse, same-sex husband/wife/spouse, opposite-sex unmarried partner, and same-sex unmarried partner."[17]

With many revisions over time, the more modern configurations of family now include both the traditional definitions found in past generations to cohabitation and non-marital childbearing models. Being single is now more socially accepted than ever before. And as both women and men choose to form households to reduce isolation and financial burdens, while not engaging in sex, it is possible to cohabitate and remain single.

It is safe to say that family is what you make of it. One important lesson holds true: If your family of origin no longer exists or if you struggle with the traditional family virtues and values to the degree that you find yourself limited or alone, it is possible to create a lifestyle that works for you. Migration, the search for a better life with a better job or environment, has displaced families to the degree that we may no longer find ourselves living in close proximity to each other. Has Grandma moved to Florida or the Southwest to get away from the snow? Even more common is the movement of the younger educated working class, especially people of color, who leave their rural lifestyles and families for urban areas where jobs with higher salaries are more plentiful.

Your friends can often become as important as your family, sometimes even more so. These relationships require the same respect and honor as others in your life. They deserve honesty, integrity, and truth. Friendship is also a reciprocal relationship, much like the impact you experience with people at work. Friends deserve your time and willingness to maintain their confidence and protection. And at the end, when the relationship is over, you need to let them go in love.

Your Family

Increasing your knowledge and the awareness of your family, its members, their attributes, their experiences, and their responses to difficulties and joys, often fills in the missing pieces that impacted your own beginning. I ask you to remember and capture the data that allows you to better understand yourself. Take a look at what *you* remember.

The exercise in the next section will help fill in any gaps that exist in the knowledge you hold about yourself and the family before you. At times, lack of communication about both the good and bad times leaves a family history open to distortion. This may require a visit, a phone call, or a text to relatives who hold the treasure of knowledge about your family. If you are lucky to still have members alive who can recall information from the past, do this work now. It may require you to ask for explanations about events from the time they lived their early lives. These are memories that remain prominent in their minds and serve as the building of their existence.

Because there is a chance that family members may perceive the world differently from one another, reach out to as many individuals as possible. Pay careful attention to any themes provided, especially anything that prompted an emotional response within you.

A Family Tree

A family tree is a diagram of personal history providing structure to an incredible number of details; it can include anything that helps you better understand yourself and your family. The possibilities are endless. But make certain that you seek out information that clarifies your story.

Here's an outline of what your family tree may include:
- Your grandparents
    - If and when they migrated to America and the circumstances surrounding their arrival
    - Countries of origin, where they lived and worked
    - Financial status
    - Religion, language
    - How they met and married
- Family and tangible losses
- Sources of pride and joy
- Your parents
    - If and when they migrated to America and the circumstances surrounding their arrival
    - Countries of origin, where they lived and worked
    - Financial status
    - Religion, language
    - How they met and married
    - Any history surrounding your parents, their siblings, and their children

- Details about your life, your spouse's history, and the lives of your children

I've outlined my own family tree to provide you with an example to use as you fill out your own.

My Family of Origin Tree

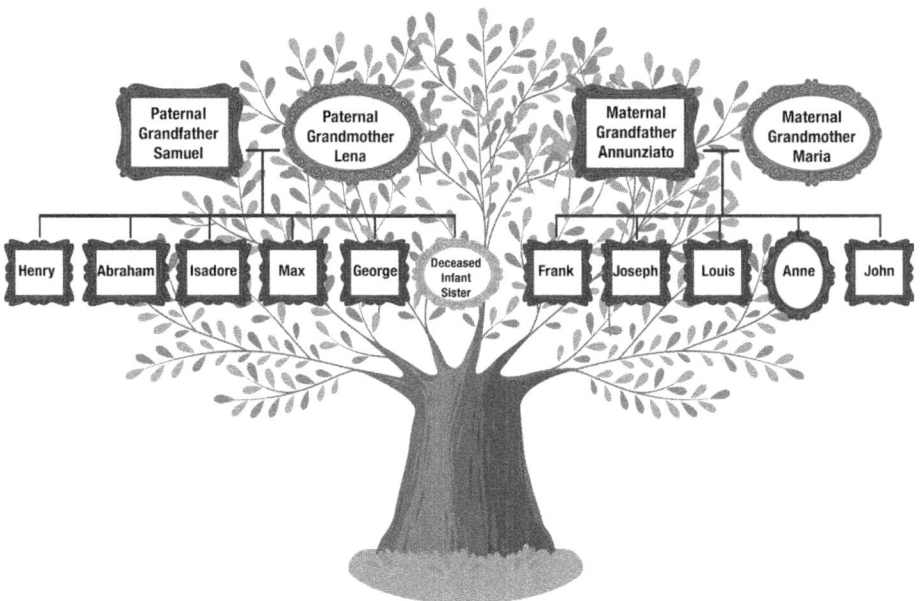

Completing Your Own Family Tree

So, what is *your* story?

Fill in your historical representation of the people you consider as family. They are individuals from your past or present who are part of your story. Seek family members who can fill in any gaps that will help you in gaining a better understanding of yourself.

Hopefully by the end of this exercise, you will be comfortable in writing your own narrative. This information can be just for you and need not be critiqued. It is to serve you and those close to you, if you allow, to see a summation of the people who participated in your development. It is most helpful to describe each person in depth and to indicate something about them that remains significant to you.

Name/relationship of family members:
_____
_____
_____

World events or special circumstances impacting family members:
_____
_____
_____

Family myths, legends, and stories:
_____
_____
_____

Situations bringing joy/pride:
_____
_____
_____

Chapter 3: We Are Family

Family events:
_____
_____
_____

Losses, divorces, death, job changes:
_____
_____
_____

Births:
_____
_____
_____

A Vision Into My Home

The family into which any of us is born and raised clearly has influence over how we perceive the world. My family was a three-generational family consisting of nine members. When I was a two-year-old, my parents moved their four children, along with my maternal grandmother and her two sisters, out of New York City to a home in Roslyn, Long Island, a suburb of New York City.

My paternal grandmother, also a widow, remained in the city and lived with her unmarried son. In those days, parents guarded over changes that caused their children to step outside of their faith and cultural beliefs. Therefore, people tended to marry within their ethnic and religious backgrounds. People of Jewish faith had strong convictions, especially after the Holocaust, about increasing the number of Jewish people in the world. Women who did not convert to Judaism could not raise Jewish children. My parents broke these rules.

My father, the son of Russian-Jewish immigrants, fell in love with my mother, an Italian-Catholic woman. They immediately faced limitations: You may remember from Chapter 1, my Jewish grandmother threatened to jump off the Brooklyn Bridge and my Italian grandmother was frightened that this decision would impact my mother's eternal salvation.

Abraham and Anne Weissman (center), married June 1, 1936

My parents never had a formal church wedding. It was simply not allowed to bring a non-Catholic to be married in the Catholic Church at the time. Instead, they got married at City Hall, and then later in the back of my grandmother's church where they were married by a Catholic priest. While he too was opposed, he agreed as long as the children would be raised Catholic.

My parents did everything in their power to live up to this. While my father never attended Sunday Mass with us, he celebrated each baptism, communion, and confirmation. In fact, when my father died and our family priest, Father Bain, arrived to offer the reciting of the Rosary, as was the custom for all Italian Catholics, his closing statement was, "Shalom, Abraham, good and faithful servant."

An important virtue was to live close to family and in a part of the city where many Italian-Americans did the same. The local Catholic Church had parish priests who could speak Italian, while the Catholic Mass was still offered in the universal Latin. Within the confines of our neighborhood, my mother's family could shop in local stores that sold items similar to those available in the "old country." Fresh Italian bread, homemade pastas, and evidence of carefully aged sausage and cheese were sold in shops near our home. This all changed when everyone became financially stable. One by one, aunts, uncles, and cousins moved to homes on Long Island.

Interestingly, my parents selected a community centered around families of Jewish background, many who shared my father's vocation in the garment industry. We were quickly identified as the outsiders.

During our first Christmas, when the entire family stepped out to decorate our home, it suddenly became clear that we were different. My father's Jewish last name had passed muster, but our nativity scene and lighted Christmas trees were a clear sign of a cultural divide. This was the beginning of my awareness of social isolation and a good reason to stay safe within the four walls of our home.

I remember being bullied and denied space in social settings. Much like a contemporary white and black blended family, all I wanted was to be accepted. My classmates had no problem reaching out for my assistance at school, but year after year, when the Sadie Hawkins dance came around, my choice for a date was quickly rejected.

The boys in my neighborhood followed the wishes of their Jewish mothers, knowing that they wouldn't be allowed to fraternize with someone who was not Jewish. The fear was that one of the boys might choose to marry outside of his faith. I must say, the Christians in town clearly thought I was Jewish based upon my last name. As a result, the rejection appeared on both sides. This was the beginning of my years being somewhat shy and anxious in social settings.

Fortunately, our home was a loving experience. Much like other Italian-American households at the time, Sunday was a celebration. It was a day of worship and a time when all family members came back to the home of their matriarch, my grandmother, for a full day of food and games. This was the one day my grandmother maintained full control of the kitchen. It all began around 6 a.m. with the simmering of meatballs, sausage, and pork for the sauce (known by many as gravy). As noted by food writer Susan Russo, "Every Italian-American woman with any pride started gravy before breakfast so it would be ready for Sunday dinner at 2 p.m."[18]

At 7:30 a.m., it was off to Mass with my mother, the four kids, my grandmother, and aunts. Then we headed back home for breakfast with my dad. Sunday dinner was like a banquet. There was an antipasto, then the pasta, followed by the roast. All five extended families and their children spent the day taking breaks from the table to play outside or to play cards.

Each time a cousin began to seriously date, the expectation was that the new person would meet the family and sit through the inquisition at Sunday dinner at my house. The younger members were careful to teach the prospective family member to pace themselves, as dinner was far more complex than American Sunday meals. Not to mention, this was a sure way to explore the person's intentions. The importance of duty to the family implanted a strong sense of attachment, belonging, and commitment. It was clear to young and old that marriage was forever. Living the life of newly emigrated Italian-Americans, the family stayed close in order to constantly reinforce values founded in religious beliefs. This meant divorce was never an option. When the offspring of this generation started to exercise independence, it created considerable stress and the need for reconciliation.

As Time Goes On: Adolescent Preparation for Emancipation

In contrast to the ways of the Italian family, one of the developmental tasks assigned to adolescents and explored by developmental scientists, is the tendency at this stage to align with others in their peer group and to emancipate from their parents. This is often a difficult time for both the child and the parents who are confounded by each other's responses. Yet, the adolescent is busy considering the value of what they learned as a child. They may choose to hold onto messages like being honest, having integrity, offering kindness to others, and taking these messages with them into the next developmental stage.

At the same time, they may want to stay out late and to engage less at home. While it can be a time of great strife in the family, this time can also be an exciting phase of experimentation and new beginnings. Adolescents in my family began to have certain privileges, like stepping away from the family dinner to take walks or share stories about their escapades of the week.

With this newer generation came an awareness of being different. This prompted the desire to shed some of the old ways and align with friends who were less entrenched in ethnic values and responsibilities.

The concept of non-attachment, also known as detachment, is a sound response to protect an individual from the emotional experience of loss during very normal developmental stages of change. This is evident during adolescence, when young adults are experimenting with different learned ways of being, including styles of behavior they may have picked up from their friends. To the family member(s) who insists that children and young adults follow the same traditions as they did, this can feel threatening.

The resolution of differences between parents and their children can at times make or break their relationships. When we accept that change is a constant, this journey ultimately becomes the cornerstone of acceptance and allows for an appreciation of differences that can be applied to other relationships. It also allows an individual to validate their own personality, values, opinions, and attitudes. When parents resist the changes in their growing children, they typically find themselves in a battle that can stifle the child's growth and their relationship with their child at this new stage.

Adolescence can be a time of considerable alienation and grief for both the teenager and the parent as they each sense a period of loss or failure. However, this is actually a time of giving up something in order to get something. The adolescent needs to shed some of the experiences of past history and take up their own. It is the job of the adolescent to figure out who they are and who they want to be, including what parts and pieces they learned growing up. The adolescent has the opportunity to choose what remains and what will be discarded. The parent has already completed their job by instilling values to the best of their ability. They may need to let go and trust that their loving presence is all their child needs.

As imagined, there are outliers in this process, as is the case when children miss the opportunity to successfully bond in their early years. Perhaps the mother or father was absent, as in the extreme cases of abandonment, to the more common experience when both parents work outside the home, or if they were perceived as abusive or neglectful. The child takes on the blame believing their parent's response was their fault.

Theorists explain magical thinking in the undeveloped mind of children, who may end up assuming they were just "not good enough." In adolescence, these children may avoid the steps to emancipate and exhibit an arrested development as they attempt to repair the relationship to get much needed attention and love. They may do so by exhibiting a longing for a parent to be more available. Or, they may act out to gain even negative attention (which is considered better than no attention at all). In this case, the child may spend years in silence trying to figure out what went wrong.

It is essential to forgive yourself. If you choose to present this awareness to your parents, hope for the best, but try not to be disappointed if they didn't see things quite the same way. They may need to defend their position as being the best they could be.

My own adolescence was fraught with a looming potential of loss due to my father's illness. I was 14 when my father was diagnosed with lung cancer. Treatment choices were extremely limited and surgery was the only option. While he survived the operation, none of us were ever quite the same after that. My father was the man who taught me to take risks and seek out adventure, the one who saved my life when at two years old, I jumped into the deep end of a pool. And now I couldn't save him. I saw a shell of a man who seemed to become more and more frightened. Yet, death and dying were never spoken and family members went about their lives.

Along with a genuine sense of isolation, I turned my attention to school, work, and the future. I graduated high school and started college with dreams of becoming a physician. I completed three years as a pre-med major, but my goal was quickly diverted when my father's cancer reemerged, this time as a frontal lobe brain tumor, making it exceptionally clear that the new reality would be to complete a baccalaureate degree as quickly as possible. On a tearful afternoon, I told my parents about my plan to change my major to nursing. They said everything I needed to hear. I felt so lost and full of grief, first at knowing I was losing my father and then at the loss of a dream.

My father died two years before I graduated college. Through the generosity of New York University's Nursing Program, with grants and scholarships, I completed my degree and, within months, passed the New York State Nursing Licensure Board Exam and went to work. Advanced degrees had to wait as I settled into life as a new nurse supporting myself in a New York City apartment.

When dealing with the loss of a loved one, so much may change that you can experience a sense of loss of control. In the middle of the work we need to do to face loss, people are often dealing with practical issues of security and feeling a lack of stability. This is especially true if the person who has died was in charge of everyday tasks.

My father's death crushed my world. It raised concerns not only about my security, but also who I might become without him to offer advice and support. I questioned if I needed to leave school or carry on. I wondered what this meant for my mother who loved this man to the very end and beyond. My reserves seemed gone until I realized the best way to honor my father was to be the achiever he taught me to be.

Chapter 3: We Are Family

While I honored my father by working hard and achieving success in my career, I grieved poorly by making bad choices in relationships. My confusion spilled over into my relationships. I had a moment where I lost my sense of worth and didn't have my guard up. I accepted people into my life who were only looking out for their own best interest.

I am telling this part of my life story not to provide an opportunity to heal—this was a time of my life that was the essence of my personal work to address in therapy. I share this information as it is quite possible that some of this information resonates with your own life story. I want to emphasize that it is possible to walk through the pain of grief and find yourself waiting on the other side. Grief changes us and sometimes the changes are so drastic that it actually adds to a sense of confusion about life in general. Grief takes a person in a whole new direction, sometimes causing extreme apprehension and doubt.

Yes, I kissed a few frogs and experienced unnecessary hurt. The loss of my father left me believing I was not good enough, or it might have been that I simply didn't have the energy to select partners who could challenge me in healthy ways. But, eventually, I discovered that everything was all right with my world. I grew to like myself and was proud of the person I had become. It was then and only then when I could actually welcome a healthy, wonderful partner, George, into my life, the man who became my husband.

It was George who taught me this different type of adult love outside of the love for family. He also taught me to be charitable and to love others. We shared the same sense of humor, a deep faith in God, and we knew almost instantly that we wanted to spend our lives together.

Since those days of early infatuation, I continued to learn what love was all about. After 40 years from our first date, George remains in my life and has faithfully walked by my side through the days and months of both good times and bad.

We declared to each other in our vows of marriage, "With all that I am, and all that I have, I honor you." So, in addition to offering each day of my work to God, asking Him to provide me with the strength and courage to help others, I also continually praise my husband for his unending love and support.

While hardly perfect, George and I base our relationship on love and honoring the many joys and challenges we've shared. We each had parents who were loving, adoring, and proud of our accomplishments. Siblings and extended family and friends have remained by our sides. We were provided the gift of two amazing sons, whom we have never once taken for granted. And now we have two incredible daughters-in-law and two grandchildren.

In 1993, I walked into the office of the American Cancer Society of Central New Jersey. I wanted to enroll in their list of therapists available to patients and families who needed support during any stage of their grief—from being newly diagnosed to dying and death. While there, I met a most unusual coordinator who took a step back and asked, "So just what is *your* story?" Instinctively I repeated that I was a nurse psychotherapist with a specialty in grief and loss and had just opened my own private practice not far away. In a somewhat gruff manner, she told me she got that part, but wanted to know my own experience with death from cancer. She quickly added the importance of knowing some of the pain firsthand.

For perhaps the first time, I fully appreciated how my family story influenced my early beginning and provided a great deal of definition to my life. I firmly believe this is the case for you, if you allow yourself to acknowledge parts of your past that created impact. Who are the people sitting on your family tree? What do you know about them? Were there significant family lessons that live on?

I want so much to give back all that I have received and more. My desire is to leave a legacy that helps my children, my grandchildren, and all of you to know that family can be a place where you can exchange thoughts and feelings freely and without judgement.

I offer you this same intent through the pages of this book in the hope that it will fill your life with peace. It is your time to recognize and appreciate your beginning. Your family is a precious place to start to better understand your journey. Take the effort to learn all that you need to learn. Revisit the memories that resound as important to you. Share them with others and be open to learning some of the things you didn't know.

Most of all, I honor you for your courage to consider a new perspective.

4

I Want to Be Somebody

So, what do you want to be when you grow up? This is a tough question for some, but my three-year-old niece, Jennifer, had it covered years ago when she proclaimed, "A dancing nurse." We all laughed at the time, but she taught us a valuable lesson in following your dream and bringing it to fruition. In Jennifer's innocence, this dream seemed totally possible and practical, a way to honor her desire for expression while having the stability and security of a desired profession. However, life often gets in the way and dreams can become clouded by reality. And, the "Jennifers" of the world are still trying to figure out this important question.

Work is the thing we do. It's often where we can pull together all that we've learned, all that we are, and all that we want to be. We can take these elements and send them into the world, demonstrating our life's purpose and meaning. Work may be the place to exercise our passion to contribute something positive to the world. It can also represent our identity. It's the place where we feel connected to our passions and to the people who share similar interests. One might say work is "who I am" as it portrays a significant part of our character.

If any of this sounds familiar, you may be tuning into the work we started earlier, when you were asked to get in touch with exactly who you are and who you want to be. This time, it's activated by the simple phrase, "What do you *do*?"

This question can follow you throughout life and may stimulate you to reach some clarity as we are a society that often bases our worth upon what we do, rather than who we are or our guiding principles. There is value in practicing your own personal elevator pitch, providing your narrative about who you are and why you do what you do. This preparation becomes extremely useful in business as it tells the world, in just a few sentences, the significance you can bring to the work environment. However, let me remind you, this is only one aspect of who you are as a whole person. When you allow yourself to know who you are at your core, you will receive clarity about how to use your engaging characteristics to not only do the work that fulfills you, but also use your ability to fill your life with loving people and relationships.

Work can be a place where you prove yourself, your abilities, and your value to someone or something bigger than you. It's where you can gain recognition from others who acknowledge that your being there provides meaning to the organization or project. It may also grant you the opportunity to appreciate your own accomplishments, giving you the chance to gauge your own credibility by what you do, and not by what others think you can do. It is especially important that you learn to define yourself rather than wait for others to do so. I suggest a combination of being practical while always incorporating your dreams.

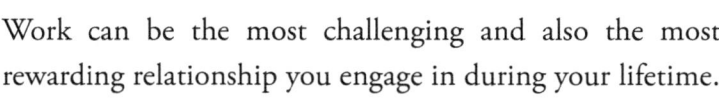

Work can be the most challenging and also the most rewarding relationship you engage in during your lifetime.

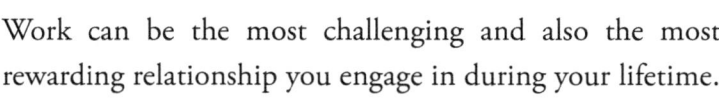

Work can provide many returns. It can fill your need to be part of a social system. It can be a microcosm of the world around us, where you learn the many views and opinions people have on current events, politics, sex, and religion, giving you the chance to see where you fit in or differ. And, work can provide financial returns and income to allow you to feel both compensated and secure. It can allow you to display your individual thinking and creativity. It may satisfy your need to feel loved, appreciated, and respected. It may be a major source of pride. And, it may give you yet another chance at being part of something with a sense of acceptance and belonging that never existed as a member of a family.

Work can provide a source of esteem and a place to carve out your niche. As you build competence and confidence, work can be a launching pad to develop other opportunities. It may even be where you receive that gentle, or not so gentle, push from your mentor encouraging you to take on new experiences. The success in accepting these new challenges can also provide a tremendous gain to your own awareness of worth. All of this is an effort for everyone to go home at the end of the day inspired by a sense of accomplishment.

Most people want to know that they have done a good job. For some positions, this is easily measured in output or production. How many loans did I approve today? How many calls did I make? For others, it is more intangible. It may be your unique style in forming social contacts or your ability to relate that makes it possible for your company to succeed. You may be diligent in appreciating the "softer" skills like remembering people's names and warmly greeting them each morning. You recognize that other people matter. And, quite likely, others are watching, learning, and admiring you from afar.

It is important to remember that, in the end, we are more alike than different. Most of us need to be needed and valued. We hope to gain trust and esteem by gaining a high regard for the work we produce. And, most of us have the same fears of rejection if we face criticism or, even worse, ridicule. Failure at our job may carry much more significance than expected as it may be part of a string of events that people silently live with, hoping for a sense of victory in at least one area of life.

Work is also the place we spend most of our waking hours. It can offer many of us the best time of our lives. But it is sometimes the place we go at the expense of time that could be spent with family or just being free. With all that said, it had better be worth it.

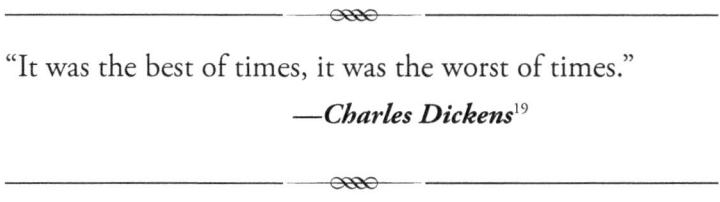

"It was the best of times, it was the worst of times."
—***Charles Dickens***[19]

With all the possibilities for successful work experiences, there are those times when things go awry. Work then becomes a source of tremendous stress. Instead of getting up in the morning eager to start your day, you may experience lethargy, disinterest, and signs of anxiety. You might even develop physical symptoms and psychophysiological illnesses like gastritis, headaches, or hypertension. These issues can result in frequent absences without you realizing that this may be a means of coping that puts your job at risk.

Experience tells us that most of these occurrences begin and end with uncertainties around expectations. In particular, clashes occur when we are surprised by changes in direction and behaviors that influence our role in the workplace. You might experience this each time there is a change in leadership. Perhaps you worked diligently to align the work you have been doing and suddenly there is a decision to eliminate all your ideas and reach a different outcome. This can be complicated by a struggle in accepting differences in style and having limited knowledge about goals.

Much of these difficulties are related to ineffective and insufficient communication, which is complicated by a lack of clarity in leadership and a culture that promotes chaos. You may want to consider the statement, "I have little trouble with the actual work I do and more difficulty with the people with whom I work, including my peers who seem invested in putting others down for their own personal gain."

Here again you are facing a "both/and" experience. "Both/and" logic serves as an alternative to a more rigid approach by Aristotle, who taught that situations are either/or and black/white. As you become open to the perspectives of others, the both/and thought process offers an opportunity to see the world with more than one solution or response. Your ability to transform your work experience rests in your own capable hands, and your willingness to collaborate with others often includes considering more than one viewpoint.

Collaboration requires preparation and expert communication to be sure the job gets done. While at the same time, it may take all you know to be able to get along and accept differences among your co-workers. It will serve both you and your organization well if your goals and those of the organization are compatible and in alignment.

You might need to consider the following:

- Are you clear about your own work goals, abilities, and ambitions?
- Do you have a sense of your employer's vision?
- Does the company's mission allow for creative expression and/or autonomy?
- Are you truly prepared to do the work?
- Are you knowledgeable about the subject?
- Why were you selected for this assignment/project?
- Is the breadth and scope of the assignment within your bandwidth? That is, do you have the time, energy, and mental capacity to tackle this job?
- What is your level of commitment, especially if it requires overtime or travel?
- Is there a project plan with due dates?
- Are you encumbered by strategic decisions or work that impacts your assignment?
- Are you clear about people and their roles?
- Do you have a trusted advisor or mentor?
- Do you understand the communication plan and how you convey progress or obstacles?
- Are you certain about the endpoint and the approval process?
- Who is the owner of the project?

Chapter 4: I Want to Be Somebody

You can appreciate how essential it is to have skills to support the nuts and bolts of the work you are expected to do each day, but you also may need to better understand how to "play in the sandbox."

When we were little and entered the sandbox, each of us brought our toys together to make roads and forts in an effort to go on an incredible journey of collaboration and fun. There were no rules, except the ones agreed upon by the group. It was a successful day if you joined others to create a space where you all could play. It felt more satisfying to work independently on a project, while having friends there to support you and provide immediate feedback, than being alone in the sandbox. You didn't care if it was praise or criticism. It was just great to be noticed. You could talk or sing or develop skills and put them to good use. You might even share ways to be more efficient in making a sandcastle. You could be spontaneous and experience pure joy or simply take pleasure in watching others as they learned to find their own way to a new creation. Still, you may have just been delighted to sit back and play in the sand. In effect, the aim of being in the sandbox was to achieve something greater than ourselves.

Today's sandbox at work can be miles away from this image. Many of us work in a cubicle or in offices that separate us by a wall or a modular partition. For some, an open office floor plan offers a sense of belonging and comfort in having people nearby to bounce off ideas and, much like the sandbox, it can be energizing and motivating as conversations may stimulate friendly competition. However, others experience this openness as over-exposure, where phone conversations or emotional states can be open for public review and intrude on the ability to concentrate and process thoughts.

And there are rules for just about everything. There are expectations about the use of the coffee pot, the age of food in the refrigerator, who fills the printer paper, the ability to take a break, coming in and leaving on time, and even an expectation to remove the trash. If you receive criticism at home for taking the last donut or failing to replace the toilet paper, rest assured that this could also happen at the office. Remember, you spend considerable time in this sandbox.

As an adult you are encumbered by responsibility and accountability. Unfortunately, you may have also lost the right to approach life with childlike innocence. It may be time to accept the challenge to understand your environment and how you find yourself there. Sometimes, it takes a great deal of your energy to be able to thrive. Only you can judge your ability to do so or whether you feel the need to leave.

The saying, "better the devil you know," conveys a message that it may be wiser and safer to remain exactly where you know the calm and stormy predicaments of your workplace, rather than venturing out into the unknown. Thus, many people choose to remain in a work setting that is familiar out of concern that the next position could prove to be equally problematic. If you are going to leave any job, do so only after you fully assess and own your part of the discontent you are experiencing. Could it actually be something about you, your work habits, or unmet expectations?

Remember, unless you are fully in touch with your own talents, limitations, and the parts of you that are still a work in progress, you bring that *you* to every setting. Once you're clear about your part of the equation, you can review your organization fairly. Do you work in an environment that lacks space to grow? What is the climate of your industry? Are there companies looking for your skills? Will you be able to achieve that one special something that you feel is missing in your present job? You likely will want to ask yourself two questions: What do I have to lose and what do I have to gain?

Each person entering the work system may have different motives or, even worse, may be unsure what is expected of them. They may have forgotten how to play nice with others and are now in a defensive posture, hoping to remain safe from criticism or the greater insecurity of being tossed out. Anger is often a defense mechanism used to keep people out.

When people fear criticism and rejection, they often present with an angry affect that keeps others at a distance.

Angry people are not hard to find at work and are more prominent in certain professions. When there is increased tension from the nature of work, as is the case with people facing life and death issues or even frequent deadlines that are perceived as such, one finds tension in the environment and an increase in lower-level efforts to cope. These may range from denial and avoidance to addiction and self-inflicting harm. It is customary to see a police officer or a soldier deny the intensity of an experience. Often, they don't have time to stop and consider the impact. The cultural norm is to hold in feelings; thus, they may not even consider the need to talk it out.

In certain settings where tensions run high, leaders frequently convene a critical incident review. This technique can be used in any setting where a shared emotional experience has the potential to cause harm to the employees and their ability to work or even cope. Staff members are asked their response to a particular event in order to encourage expression of thoughts, feelings, unresolved issues, or regrets.

While seeming restricted to certain professions, this approach could be extremely helpful in any job where people face a great deal of stress that can accumulate over time. Sadly, the default behavior of many people in the workplace is to just make it through another day without acknowledging these stressors and feelings. Or, they simply don't have the energy or support to resolve instances that have occurred.

It has been established by neurobiologists that emotional stress can be stored at the cellular level. When left unattended, individuals may release these emotions when they least expect it. Or, they may accumulate the stress until organs and systems within the body are affected. At times, being in an environment shaped by anger, fear, and guilt becomes toxic to the point that all employees are affected. They then develop a style of collusion to purposely avoid detection and to maintain an equilibrium that enables them to continue to do their jobs.

This behavior is not unique to these professions but can be seen when an individual is in a situation where he or she has lost the ability to resolve a threatening situation. It can happen when a small business owner over-invests in inventory and suddenly feels impotent to changes in the economy that cause a decrease in sales. The anxiety of failure becomes central to their being. This can also happen when a co-worker or person in leadership begins criticizing you or the work you do on a regular basis. While this is often a projection of the person's own sense of failure, it takes a great deal of fortitude to rise above these events.

Situations like these happen more frequently than one might imagine and require an investment in oneself to begin to disengage from the experience. In some cases, individuals may face symptoms of post-traumatic stress disorder (PTSD), which can include anxiety, depression, pain, withdrawal, irritability, guilt, shame, and numbing. These symptoms are monumental and typically require professional assistance.

Is it a Heart, Lung, or a Kidney?

Each of us have requirements, rules, and deadlines that can add to our work experience. Some of us may have several supervisors or adjunct staff asking for work to be done to help support their workload. As a result, a means of self-preservation is an essential skill to pick up along the way.

While working on a project for a large Los Angeles hospital system, I often found myself running into the office of the administrative assistant, Tina, begging her to help me reach a deadline. She was a direct report to several directors and hardly had a free moment in her eight-hour day. As a result, she had to learn ways to prioritize and still not offend anyone needing her help. In time, I anticipated her response and could laugh with her when she asked, "Is it a heart, a lung, or a kidney?" Tina used this technique to place the responsibility on the person requesting her aid. In time, she learned to trust me when I said, "Today it is a heart. Please do your very best to get this back by close of day."

So how do we learn to cope? First of all, it is important that we select a job or profession that is realistic and meaningful to us. Then we need to be sure we have the preparation required. If you go to work worrying someone will find you have been dishonest and really don't have the skills to do the job, something needs to be addressed to correct this. The groundwork includes the development of a *self* who can live the characteristics necessary to engage in the work, no matter how challenging and unpredictable. In essence, to accomplish the work requirements, you must put all of your ducks in a row in order to be the most authentic person you can be. Those with consistent success are those who have honed in on their engaging qualities that make them not only attractive, but necessary to a company.

Honesty, integrity, and a willingness to go the extra mile are all admirable characteristics of successful people. These employees become proficient in high-level communication skills that include mastery of verbal and written communication. Also important to most positions is the need to be respectful by showing an interest in others while understanding and honoring boundaries. In general, these qualities support an inner circle that can be very valuable and rewarding. The ability and willingness to share, to mentor, and to be present are some of the most compelling qualities of a work relationship.

Work Culture

The norms around work and work culture are ever-evolving and employees are taking greater leadership in making work the gratifying place it can be. Most people agree that when the culture is one of acceptance with a willingness to respect new ideas, employees tend to be more productive. Today's workforce primarily consists of Baby Boomers and Millennials.

Leaders are realizing the vast difference when they establish relationships that are authentic, with open communication and consistency in approach. This behavior replaces a more traditional leadership style in which all changes come from the top. Rather than remaining separate from the workforce, leaders are identifying a benefit to being open to new possibilities by establishing processes to vet ideas and reach agreement together. Also, the greater the sense of ownership in one's business, the greater the opportunity for unlimited productivity, creativity, and commitment. Therefore, asking employees to run their business or part of the business as if it was their own has boundless rewards.

Treat this company as if it were your own.

Despite all this, when uncertain work cultures are permitted, it may encourage human behavior to revert to old ways. As a new person enters a work environment, they may be scrutinized by others during the "getting to know you" period. There is always a possibility that a change in the system can raise fear and insecurity in others, a condition over which you may have little control. Their knowledge and competence may become a threat to peers.

Employees may consider the new arrival as a burden or another task, as orientation often falls on everyone's shoulders. Any one of us in this situation has choices about how we proceed. If you are working to improve your communication, take responsibility for the way in which you communicate and present yourself to others. Demonstrate a willingness to share vital information that will help the new person in their work. Any one of us, including the newest employee, can improve upon a culture by establishing a willingness to add to the knowledge already present.

A very wise professor of mine once said that the best thing a new employee can do when entering a new work environment is to stop everything and "watch the way the wind blows." Meaning, take time to understand the rules, responsibilities, traditions, and customs among the people within the culture. She also underlined the importance of knowing the true leaders whether or not their title represents their level of responsibility. Specifically, your job is to understand the leadership, both assigned and informal. While it is assumed that the directors and the CEO are in charge, it may be the administrative assistant who holds the most clout in the department.

According to an article by Kate Heinz, new employees are often unaware of the actual culture upon arrival.[20] Experience tells us that within the approved culture, there are often outliers operating by their own rules. This can cause you to question whether you have made the right choice.

Common findings include:

- Disparities in leadership goals

- "Interdependency-based" conflict when departments are operating as silos without appreciating the work of others
- Differences in productivity and expectations
- Cultural-based dissension with either language or cultural differences making it difficult to relate or to be included
- Personality clashes with public demonstrations of differences
- Loud working environments making it difficult to concentrate
- Limited opportunities to be recognized
- The reputation of the company is questionable
- High turnover rate

The following diagram provides a summary of some of the major sources of conflict at work. While the responsibility seems to weigh heavily on the organization and its leaders, a company is only as good as the people who are present to do the work.

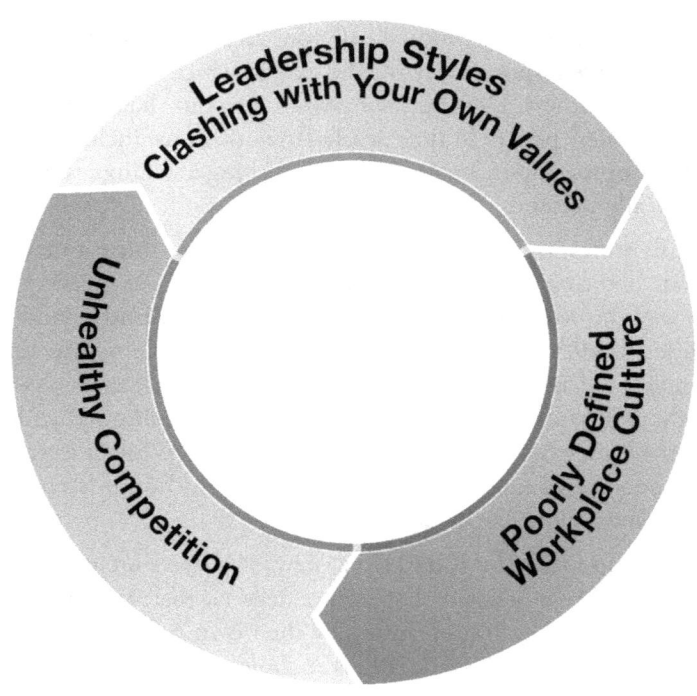

An employer may not recognize the importance work can play on an individual. However, employment represents establishing relationships that are central to your life. To make work fulfilling, the ideal situation is to take responsibility and seek clarity in all of the engaging qualities that impact your success. As a responsible employee, it is essential to acknowledge your own vision and how well your opinions, values, and beliefs can be incorporated into the tasks and expectations of work. You may need to take time to discern how freely you can contribute ideas or exercise creativity. If creativity isn't one of your personal values, determine what is important to make or break your work experience.

In turn, each organization publishes and, hopefully lives by, a series of documents known as the Mission, Vision, and Value Statements. These documents are generally released during the orientation period with an expectation that you, the employee, lives up to the "company way." But wouldn't it be better to gain a glimpse of the organization's traits much earlier, even during the interview phase? Then, you as the potential employee could determine with some certainty if your personal values, visions, and goals are in sync with the company's. Only you can decide if you are willing to make certain compromises.

Your Desired Work Experience

Take a moment and consider the qualities of your work experience that are most important to you. Which functions do you enjoy the most and which would you prefer to eliminate? Prioritize your list and areas of compromise. Consider that any of these goals will require direct, honest, and open communication.

Here are some questions that may help:

- Do you have a standard work schedule? Are you given ample notice if there is a change?
- Do you expect to be considered for an annual raise?
- Can you only work the day shift?
- Does the company ever downsize due to times of low production? How is it determined who would go home?
- Are there company-wide celebrations?
- Are employees expected to work additional hours without pay, e.g., work through lunch?

There is a measure of reciprocity when an employee enters into a contract with their employer. This is why it is so important that you understand the nature of your work, what is expected, and whether your skills are a good match. If something is in question or raises doubt, now is the time to speak up.

A problem can occur when a person avoids communication or when they need validation that they are on track with their ideas and the plan of action. Some people accept a position hoping they can quickly learn what they need to learn. This knack is actually rare, resulting in a workforce that is full of novices. If you are seeking an entry level position, all is good. However, if you are expected to arrive at the board room on your second day with ideas and observations, be certain that you can live up to your part of the commitment.

Whatever we choose to do in the area of work requires commitment, energy, discipline, enthusiasm, and, more importantly, responsibility and accountability. This is the given, but not always within the employee/employer's understanding. When accountability and responsibility are missing from either side of the relationship, it may be doomed from the start.

Responsibility is being answerable or responsive to something within your control. The person responsible is generally charged as the author of a decision or occurrence. Regrettably, if not a learned value through early development, employees may take issue with being held responsible and accountable.

Responsibility includes the capacity for moral decision-making, which in turn requires rational thought or action. On a simplistic basis, the average employee is at the very least agreeing to attend all required meetings, being dependable in accomplishing tasks in a timely manner, and conducting business with integrity and honesty. Being accountable is only slightly different as it focuses more on what others may expect. It includes judgement for the success or failure of a decision, or the choices agreed upon and the obligation to report and explain. The individual is then answerable for consequences of the direction of a plan or business decision.

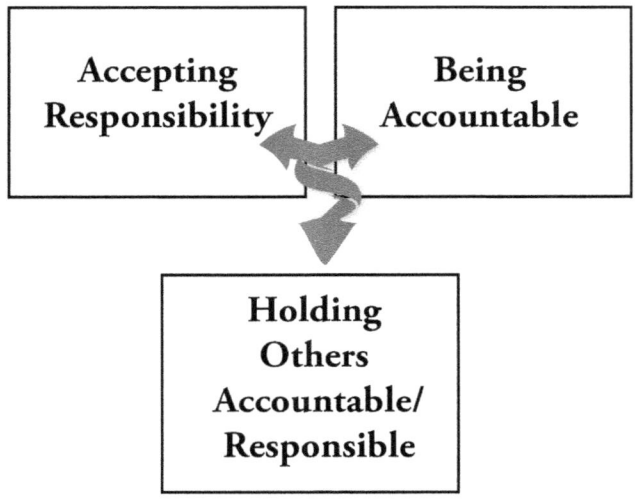

This is a good time to ask yourself about your own work experience:

- Is there a culture supporting a fair assessment of new and current employees?
- Do interviews occur with only the hiring manager or do staff working in the same position have an opportunity to participate?
- Is there an atmosphere that promotes training and growth?
- Is this a culture of acceptance? Are there any obvious restrictions?
- How do leaders view your contribution?
- Is there a regular forum to discuss the work you do?
- Do annual evaluations reflect your ability to perform?
- What is the nature of the relationships in the office? What about with leadership?
- Are you free to speak your true thoughts and feelings, or are you guarded?
- Do employees readily support leadership or does undermining of authority occur?
- If you disagree with a new plan or policy, how do you choose to handle it?

Open and Honest Communication

Years ago, a wonderful story describing the work ethic of geese was presented at a conference. The author proposed that we might have an ideal world if people behaved more like geese. As is true of geese, one might find it important for people to share a common direction and a sense of community. The belief is that employees and leaders could get where they are going quicker by traveling on the strength of each other rather than being in constant competition. The story suggested staying in formation with those in charge and giving our help as needed, offering criticism only for the purpose of building support and encouragement.

Today, one often finds the opposite. Individuals hope their efforts will receive the top appraisal, as evaluations often translate into financial rewards. Today we often find chatter spoken in staff lounges and private meetings that may never rise to the attention of leadership. These side conversations have the dangerous propensity to radically change the tone of the environment.

Emerging companies are recognizing a shift that encourages open communication. The current thinking is that work culture needs to ensure that each member perceives some measure of success. It is quite useful to encourage team members to address concerns openly with the right people present. On the other hand, the total shutdown of communication and following a *loose goose* might devastate a company.

I think back to my days as a nursing director: Our monthly meetings often came to a halt when one or more of my colleagues would voice their concern about the balance of power among department leadership. A favorite nursing leader had resigned and many directors were vying for their position, making certain they were not left out.

Introducing additional staff also changes the environment. It is well-known that new employees go through a kind of "honeymoon period." During the "honeymoon," people are expected to explore and learn how to be in an intimate relationship where there is compromise along with acceptance of ideas. New employees benefit from the wiser, more senior staff offering their perspective and wisdom on typical work tasks. If encouraged, staff can seek each other out for support and act as a sounding board to solutions.

Many of us realize that people have different needs when it comes to recognition and appraisal. Some people only need private recognition as a positive force toward the success of project completion. Some appreciate public displays of their contribution. For others, gaining a percentage of cost savings or adding to the bottom line becomes their best motivator. The most effective leader takes the extra effort to understand what matters to everyone in the working environment. While each person may be assigned similar work, there may be differences in what they need in order to accomplish their work and how they want to be recognized for it.

Being given the privilege of serving as both a leader and a team member in different circumstances, I gained an appreciation for the support I could provide my staff. In fact, my best effort in these relationships was in working to understand the individual and finding a personal way to demonstrate my belief in their ability to be a star. Fortunately, this came easy to me as I truly enjoyed meeting people where they were in their personal and professional development. It required an entire series of events including hiring the right people, having the right people in the right positions, and then supporting them as they learned. When certain individuals were marginal in their participation, it caused the greatest angst in finding something for which they could be rewarded.

It was then that I became determined to treat all my employees the same. To begin this journey, I held to a position that I would only do half the work in our relationship. The employee and I met, sometimes frequently, to discuss their part and my part. In doing so, they assumed more control until a feeling of confidence emerged and they were able to complete the work at hand.

"Treat people as if they were what they ought to be, and you help them to become what they are capable of being."
—*Johann Wolfgang von Goethe, philosopher, poet, playwright*

In truth it is not always just about believing in people. It is also important to be a role model and to teach people how to behave in these difficult times. Not only do people lack the education around responsibility and accountability, they struggle to find models in their leadership that are acceptable to their own personal values. We respond best to a culture that embraces and encourages responsibility and ensures that all are held to the same level of expectation.

As a leader, I often had employees come to me for help solving a problem. Rather than giving the easy answer, I often asked them to explore their own intuitive response. I learned that instead of providing a quick solution, it was far more advantageous to ask them to study the options and return with a justification for the choice they believed served the purpose. The underlying message supported a basic leadership tenet allowing the employees to experience a leader who believed in their ability and competence. This action also encouraged responsibility, confidence, and ownership that enabled each of them to take on their own leadership style. In life there are many correct choices, but it takes practice to find them and to evaluate what works best for any given situation.

We all need to take time to consider our own guiding principles. This is the idea that each of us is responsible for our own success. To be able to take credit for your own success, it is essential that you articulate a set of beliefs that define who you are and how you want the world to see you.

Feel free to align yourself with any of my personal ideologies, as they have served me well:

- All people may not have been created equal but have the same opportunities to exercise choices that can provide them an equal position in this world.
- I choose to treat people as I would like to be treated.
- Set life priorities: Faith, family, and work.
- Recognize when something is bigger than you and requires help.
- Begin each day with a spirit of gratitude.
- Acknowledge the people who support me and give credit where credit is due.
- Honor the gift of knowledge that enables me to achieve the work I do.
- Work hard and play hard.
- If at first you don't succeed, try, try again.
- Don't count your chickens before they are hatched.
- Acknowledge errors.
- Love what you do.
- Send out love and it will return in multiples.

Many have experienced work environments where employees are treated as if they are disposable. Also, many have an awareness that large corporations no longer reward staff for their years of loyalty and service. Instead, some enact layoffs to avoid paying higher salaries or eliminate employees with pensions.

Employees need to understand ways to be most valuable to a company. Take this as an opportunity to learn. Leaders need to advocate a level of transparency to support individual growth in their people. Working for a company needs to once again feel like a privilege. With this privilege comes commitment from all sides. Therefore, staff need to be assured that if they work diligently and efficiently in an effort to be productive, they will be rewarded. When factors are such that the company is failing and decisions to lower the workforce are essential, all staff members need to experience a sense of fairness.

While most leaders want to believe that their staff is passionate about the work they do, passion may be poorly understood, especially when it is not part of a person's experience. It is important to acknowledge that the vast majority of individuals don't take time to think about passion in relationship to work. For many, education is a means to an end. For some, education serves as a stepping stone to applying what they've learned.

Too often, we hear people say that they left college unprepared to start any job. The vision of being a professional "somebody" may have been misleading. While wanting to live the American dream and to reach a sense of fulfillment upon graduation, leaving school may actually be just the beginning of the path. That first job is the time to learn how to negotiate the real world, earn money, and pay bills. It is also a time to notice what it takes to be viewed as unique and a genuine service to a company.

As a result, we find some individuals who excel, some who maintain the status quo, and others who do as little as possible to avoid being noticed or confronted. Once again, work environments tend to occupy most of our waking hours and should be a source of joy and gratification. Employers have a responsibility to be fair and to hold each employee accountable for doing their part in bringing value to the company. Since this is a reciprocal relationship, employees are accountable to the company and their peers to collaborate fairly to reach company and individual goals.

When all this fails, as it will from time to time, it is important to have developed the skills to communicate needs and wants and to present your case to the correct people. Each of us needs to be able to ask a question or offer a suggestion to people who may actually have the authority to make change. Each employee needs to be able to act with integrity and ask what can be done to demonstrate that their contribution added to the whole.

Ask yourself:

- What did you do today to make your work environment or culture a better place?
- Did you support a value that you all need to work effectively together?
- Were you able to resolve a problem arising from a conflict that slowed down the team's effectiveness or your ability to do your work?
- Was there an opportunity for you to demonstrate that you have the capacity to work diligently and more than just the bare minimum?
- Have you considered any opportunities to mentor others to improve the end result of the work product, as well as, adding to the experience of the individual?
- Have you considered creating opportunities for others to achieve recognition?
- Do you promote acceptance and equality?

Equality in the Workplace

Equality is such a simple word, yet it often escaped my awareness while growing up. It seemed quite normal to live in a house full of older people, with our extended family joining in to celebrate on the weekends.

Earlier, I described social differences in being born to a family of Russian-Jewish and Italian-Catholic heritages. This carried its own stereotypes. Yet, I did not have to address the issue of being a different color and I am hardly the expert on this subject today. I know that my African American colleagues still struggle and remain constantly mindful of inequities they have experienced. I am especially struck and terrified for our world when I hear incidences of racial profiling where innocent people are attributed with a different set of rules than those of us who appear to be white. It reminds me of another time during World War II when we learned people were extinguished in gas chambers because of their faith, their appearance, or their ethnicity.

Your part can be to continue to promote acceptance based not on the color of a person's skin, but on their achievements and the characteristics that make each individual unique. I have heard close friends describe that they are always vigilant and feel a need to work harder to be accepted simply because of their race.

As a woman, this is also the case. Little did I know that I would have to work harder to prove myself. I fully admit that I met women who openly informed me they were attending college to get their *Mrs.* and it didn't much matter to them whether they had a high grade point average or GRE score. In fact, I had no idea how quickly my own life would change simply by being a woman.

I got my first taste of inequality in the workplace at New York University when a Mammalian Anatomy instructor whispered in my ear, "You must know that staying in the pre-med curriculum is going to prevent one of the guys in the class from getting into med school." I was outraged that this man would suggest that I was preventing someone else from achieving his dream, but I pushed that idea away and moved onto the task at hand. It was much later, when I was a nursing director of five unique hospital service lines, that I realized there were clear obstacles to success solely based on my gender.

One such obstacle was when I was invited to a budget preparation meeting for the next fiscal year. The director of finance appeared in a room of selected directors whom he determined could help streamline the process. The first set of information provided was an extensive list of salaries for all employees. This seemed fairly cut and dry as my nursing staff's salaries were measured on licenses and certifications, education, and years of experience. However, thumbing through the massive green data sheets, I spotted the salary of a pharmacy director who was earning $100,000 more than any of the nursing directors. We had a similar background and years of experience. In my usual manner, I privately asked the question. I was advised that there were many factors of inequity, but this one was because the individual was a man. I could not leave this information without talking to my supervisor, the COO, who was also a woman.

Unfortunately, the advice I received was rather astounding. "There are things you must learn to accept," she said. "Learn to be a gopher and keep your head down." With a heavy heart, I eventually left this position for a role that could expand my client system and for which I could feel compensated with a salary that matched my value to the corporation. The path I took allowed me to continue to respect what I valued and believed, but it meant leaving that which I loved to do and entering a whole new world where I would have to prove myself once again. This was a life-changing experience, but I knew that my only course of action was to leave.

Women were traditionally viewed as an auxiliary part of a male-dominated world where men were the breadwinners and women's primary responsibility was in the home creating a comfortable environment and bearing children. For example, the belief once was that women were too emotional to be in higher leadership positions. After all, it was deemed that their emotions were out of control at least once a month and then later during menopause. This was a vestige of a former time. Perhaps the lesson here is that we can learn from each other. Develop a case and speak your truth. Be accountable for your part. And, recognize that the world is also changing.

The best advice I can offer you is to rise above inequality. Whether you are facing inequalities as a member of the LGBTQ community, or if you are a person of color, or a woman, be the person you want to be. Not everyone is a fighter for human rights, but there are many willing to do so. Align yourself with them. There is no value in sitting back and feeling angry about a condition that may be bigger than you. Above all, be cautious about using this issue as a reason to be bitter. Don't let it paralyze you. By doing so you are only proving a point that has been used against individuals over the years.

As human beings on the cusp of change, we are challenged to have it all. By carefully communicating a vision and plan, make certain you ask for and receive the support and the buy-in needed to make this possible. Communication is a major factor to success as the changes in lifestyle need to be clearly spelled out. A change in your role creates a change for the entire family and your work environment.

I ask you to believe in yourself. Be a gopher at times *if and when* you are simply not feeling safe, but rise again. Be certain that you have all your requirements in order. You owe it to yourself to develop the necessary knowledge and the academic and work experience that supports your ability to stand alongside anyone else. This will clear your own fears of inadequacy and build the confidence that you, the authentic you, are capable of doing the job and worthy of receiving recognition.

Make certain that you are truly prepared through education and experience to seek the assignments that are compatible with your interest and goals. Do your homework to find out all you need to know about the actual positions that are available. When you have created skills that are unique, carve out a role that meets the needs of the organization and prove it by demonstrating improvements to the bottom line.

If the bottom line is money, you will need to prove your case by increasing revenue. If your organization is invested in changing the culture, show how your role will assist to reach adaptive ways of functioning. You have a responsibility to yourself to rewrite your script and to challenge the myths and storytelling that occurs around the ability of women and others in the workforce. Whenever facing indications that you may be different, embrace those parts of you—they may be exactly what the company needs. Reinterpret the myth and show how you are essential. Individuals can and will continue to thrive in organizations as they learn to tell their story in a different voice.

Some of us exist by simply having too much of life on our plates. Perhaps you start your day by preparing lunches and getting children off to daycare or school. Or, you may find yourself as a member of the "sandwich generation" with both young children and older family members who require care. It is possible to juggle these responsibilities by learning to compartmentalize. This is an active behavioral approach to be the best you can be at work and also at home. It encourages you to separate the responsibilities that are present each day. It will take extensive preparation and communication as you will want support from a variety of resources. You remain highly accountable for each area of your life, but it is possible to live both lives without guilt.

When at home, do your best to be totally present and do the best job any person can do in meeting and exceeding household and family responsibilities. When at work, separate yourself from worry as you have people and things in place to assure safety and security for your family members. Let your children grow to be the capable people they need to be. Allow your partner to be the partner you hope to have.

> When we fail to engage in a crucial conversation, every aspect of our lives can be affected—from our careers, to our personal lives, and even our health.

Again, your ability to transform your experience at work to a successful one rests in your hands. You may need to increase your knowledge on the subjects related to communication and how to successfully engage in crucial conversations. This will be covered in greater detail in Chapter 6, "Finding the Words to Say." For now, you may need to let yourself be a known entity to your leadership, who typically appreciate knowing their rising stars. Let yourself step out of your comfort zone and be different. Be courageous and allow things to happen that will serve as building blocks to your confidence and success.

You bring incredible uniqueness to the table including your skills and your ability to perceive issues and problems differently. Your style may be different and may not always be fully understood, but it will make others sit up and become aware that you are someone to contend with.

With these tools in hand, sit back and watch how the joy of bringing honesty and integrity actually works in your favor.

5

It's All About Love

You may recall a great deal of discussion about the development of *self* as it has followed you through the pages of this book. Hopefully upon arrival you recognized yourself as a member of a family, living under the shelter of a life offering stability and safety. Your family's beliefs, values, and traditions instinctively became yours as easily as knowing exactly what to serve for Thanksgiving dinner. And so it is that all children have an instinctual desire to connect. That connection is at our very core. We feel it, sense it, and can name it, but cannot always sustain it. In each and every relationship, love requires a steadfast consciousness to remain in touch with, not only our precious *self*, but also an enduring devotion to be continuously in tune with the needs, wants, and desires of others.

The moment your body chemistry sent a signal to your mother's womb that it was time for your birth, labor quickly followed, and everyone prepared for this great event. With each pain came progress through the three stages of birth until one of your body parts made its way out of the birth canal. It could have been an arm, a leg or even your rear end. When your head presented, someone announced, "I see caput," a statement alerting the delivery team that labor is progressing. Then, an intensity began with all members in the room, each holding their breath waiting for evidence of life and that first cry. The umbilical cord was cut, a quick assessment made, and you were placed on your mother's body, skin-to-skin. You were no longer cramped inside and floating in that home of amniotic fluid. Your little eyes tried to peer open to see this new place and to listen for familiar voices. And, for the very first time in your life, you experienced love and intimacy.

This was the start of a lifetime voyage. Much like the brightness of a new star, a baby gives us another chance to be renewed. It is a time of empowerment for both the mother and father who now recognize their achievement in creating this incredible being. Parents find a whole new way to love and often take the time to rekindle a vow to make this child's life even better than the life before them. You possessed an intrinsic desire to be part of something, to belong, and to be accepted. Yet, at this moment in your life, your only responsibility was to breathe.

The birth experience was an introduction into the world of people who hopefully were prepared to provide for you until you could provide for yourself: To love you without condition, care for your every need, and provide you with the sense that you are safe and secure. Reality often strikes when a couple, albeit fresh out of childbirth class, takes their baby home and asks, "Now what do we do?" It's true that babies don't come with an owner's manual and families are not always as prepared as they wish, but even the most challenging experiences have a way of sorting themselves out without permanently harming a child and sending them straight to years of therapy. And why? Because given any circumstance, people try to make the very best choices.

Types of Intimacy:
Things that Foster Closeness and Connection

We know that the concept of intimacy takes many forms—from the experience of childbirth and throughout the passage of life. Despite this, for some the suggestion of intimacy stirs up some unfamiliar sense of wild sexual encounters and one-night stands. On the contrary, intimacy comes in several dimensions and is a basic human desire that's as significant as that first experience in the birthing room. You may be considering the opportunities for physical intimacy where handholding, kissing, hugging, and sexual touch are an active expression of a desire to experience closeness.

But physical intimacy is only one type. People engage in emotional intimacy by giving cues about their emotional state and feelings. Mental intimacy can happen whenever you find yourself sharing the same views or visions or in the midst of an intelligent conversation on a subject that holds meaning to you and others.

In a similar manner, individuals may experience a sense of intimacy when a heated disagreement reaches resolution where the parties involved realize their connection is more important than their differences. You may also find a sense of spiritual intimacy when seeking inner peace. You might find solace in the ability to respect and be respected for a shared purpose or belief and exercise that dimension of intimacy through meditation and prayer.

Chapter 5: It's All About Love

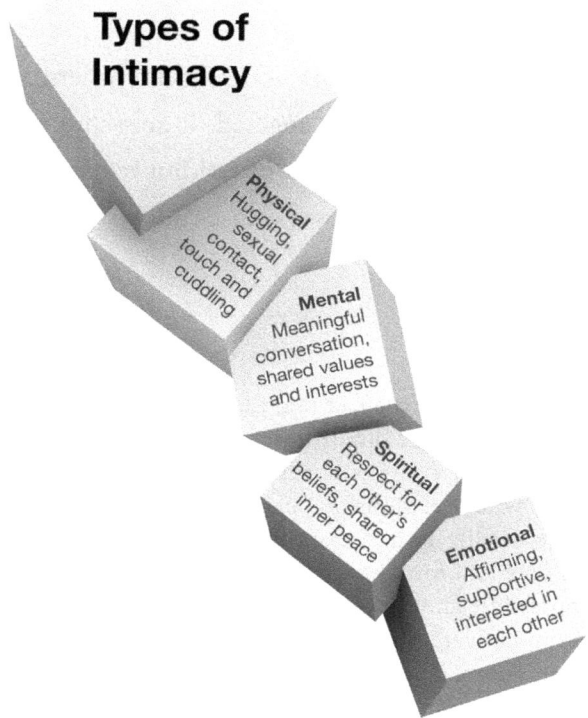

Love and intimacy know no bounds. We have the capacity to experience both throughout our lifespan although many may admit that the nature of love changes over time. In infancy, we receive love in the meeting of needs: Feeding, changing a child's diaper, and spending time soothing a crying infant, all demonstrating a level of involvement and attention at an early age. One might argue that a baby lacks a cognitive awareness of love, yet during this time of innocence and vulnerability, I am quite certain that a child recognizes the warmth and comfort of being loved. In some ways, it may be more complex as we age, but in many ways, it is the same.

How do we find a suitable way to explain and define love? Quora, an internet website, asks the question, "How would you define love?" After a series of extremely poignant suggestions, love is believed to be one of the most talked about subjects throughout the world, while at the same time, hard to define. Clarence Sherrick, a self-described metaphysician, tells us it is an energy of spirit, much like fire that both stimulates and consumes the soul.[21] Love is also the subject of a well-known passage in the Bible that's popularly used in wedding ceremonies.

> Love is patient, love is kind. It does not envy, it does not boast, it is not proud. It does not dishonor others, it is not self-seeking, it is not easily angered, it keeps no record of wrongs. Love does not delight in evil but rejoices with the truth. It always protects, always trusts, always hopes, always perseveres.[22]

Yes, "love is patient" despite the fact that life presents many challenges. You can either view these challenges as opportunities to learn more about yourself and others or perceive each life event as a crisis that stops you from living and loving that person before you. Relationships can be rich in disagreement, especially when there are two intelligent and emotional human beings both trying to meet their needs to be accepted for what they believe, to be understood, and to safely express their impression and viewpoint. These disagreements can seem benign and can range from conversations about the style of food at a restaurant to how you decorate your home. These less serious disagreements can be viewed as a testing ground for you to learn how to manage differences without leaving anyone bleeding. There may be a lot of energy placed on these subjects, but in truth there is no harm, no foul. They prepare you for the more significant differences you will face down the road. Differences such as the insecurity around each other's friends or family, whether to start a family or choose to be child-free, your choice in parenting style, or deciding to accept the dying and death of a loved one.

Remember, love "is not easily angered and does not dishonor others." My best suggestion is to take a breath, a big step back, and remember what this person means to you. Is this disagreement the hill to die on? No one is perfect, and the behavior that occurs when you engage in a battle trying to be "right" can be one of many that chips away at the wholeness of your union.

Having said this, it is not all or nothing or black and white in which one person in the relationship must always relinquish control. It is inevitable that we will face situations where you need to pick your battles and truly consider the importance of the situation before you. You may need to ask yourself whether the disagreement is significant enough to step away from a relationship or whether there is room for repair.

Many people have been hurt and disappointed over time, leaving them wary of taking a chance in starting a new relationship. You may feel wounded and doubt your ability to love and be loved. It is reasonable that you may take measures to protect yourself and have even become guarded trying to avoid the potential of more hurt. There is a tendency to become closed off to everyone, which only reinforces a false belief that you are better off by yourself. The thing you may fail to recognize is that every one of us has the innate desire to be connected and to feel the joy and comfort of love and intimacy. That being said, loving someone requires a level of risk, as well as an ongoing commitment to work at the relationship. Here again, it is one of life's lessons where you are giving up something in order to get something. At this point in time, you may have to let down your barriers; connecting at this level of intimacy requires you to enter a place of vulnerability.

Let me offer encouragement that each time you face a new or difficult circumstance, do all that you can to search deep inside yourself to explore the meaning. Try your best to understand what, if anything, is being laid out before you to learn. Much like the child within you, taking this effort facilitates an awareness of your untapped wisdom. Take time to write about your experiences or seek out someone who serves as your trusted advocate. Who could this person be? Is this your "Paraclete," your trusted advisor, your mentor, or someone in close proximity to you? It may change given the circumstance; you may need someone to support you through your work and professional life as well as someone who can support you in your personal life. As we say in Gestalt therapy, let yourself explore situations and then separate out the thoughts and feelings that affect you. Become more aware of feelings that appear when allowing yourself to explore new ways of being. Mastering life's difficulties are within your capable hands. Become more intimately involved with all that you are and all that you are capable of being. Give yourself more credit in your ability to love and interface within a complex, changing world.

You do not live in a vacuum, so give credence to what is occurring in your life. Take into consideration all that is happening. When a relationship lacks love and intimacy, or something has diminished over time, people go through the same process of realizing loss as if someone has died. This includes a period of denial and anger. You have experienced a loss. Let's call it what it is and allow yourself to properly grieve. Out of your grief may come many questions. You may ask, "What did I do or didn't do to make this happen?" This question is likely the by-product of an emotion called guilt.

Human beings, especially women, are so advanced in the acceptance of guilt, even when it isn't ours to own. It is time to recognize that no one has all the responsibility or power to make or break a relationship. No amount of accepting things that you know intuitively are not quite right will improve the outcome. In fact, failure to put concerns into words may be one of the deadliest behaviors that can contribute to the demise of a relationship.

Communication at least gives you a fair chance of gaining awareness into yourself and your partner. If you proceed without taking that chance and you go on to ask, "Why me?" you may be getting closer to being in touch with your anger and disappointment, yet another part of your grief. Perhaps this question will support the work that you need to do to gain clarity, while evaluating what it is you want and need in a relationship. Let yourself be clear about what you bring to the table, what you expect in a partner, and most importantly, how each of you define love.

In the Broadway show, *Fiddler on the Roof*, Tevye asks his wife, Golde, whether she loves him. How do any of us truly know for that matter? Her answer is of great value as love is not only a state of being, or a feeling, but clearly a demonstration of actions and behaviors.

When love exists in a relationship, allow it to be defined and determine if it meets the needs of both members of the relationship. If this definition is failing the perception of either of the couple, take this as a challenge worth addressing. Sometimes, providing a roof over your partner's head or food on the table is simply not enough, especially when you have it in you to do more. A person may be looking for a kind word, a sense of appreciation, or a moment that makes time stand still.

What do you expect from love?

_____
_____
_____
_____
_____
_____

What do you provide to your partner in your current relationship?

_____
_____
_____
_____
_____
_____

Chapter 5: It's All About Love

What does he or she receive from you?

_____
_____
_____
_____
_____
_____
_____

What, if anything, do you lose by being in this relationship?

_____
_____
_____
_____
_____
_____
_____

Finding Your Way to Intimacy

As an infant, from that first moment you learned what it felt like to be loved without question of being good enough, you also learned that your fingers and toes were mysteriously part of your body and that, with practice, you could control their movement. While some of you will find this insignificant, consider the fact that your ability to touch and move served as a precursor to your survival. Feeding is actually a tremendous step—it not only represents the ability to take in food and water, but it also predicts a child's ability to comfort and soothe him or herself when no one else is around, not to mention the confidence it builds in conquering another milestone. With practice, human beings can do just about anything. This includes finding your way to intimacy.

Even the youngest of us begin to adapt and eventually realize independence by reaching into some primitive place that supports development and growth. With enough support from your environment and a belief in yourself that you are capable, the world of possibilities continues to open up to you and reinforces positivity within you. I see this in young children in even the simplest occasions when they find something entertaining and receive feedback indicating that others share their joy.

This occurs into adulthood—welcoming other people, colleagues, and friends into your life who appreciate your humor, your intellect, and your aura, which surrounds you and encourages others to want to be close to you. We actually begin to learn about our ability to sustain life, make choices, and thrive by a multitude of experiences with people, not only those associated with you by virtue of genetics.

Early in my undergraduate nursing education, I realized that dying patients were placed at the end of a hospital hall with the doors tightly closed. I started to question this behavior and asked just when do our needs for intimacy end? To me, this behavior reinforced that "dying people have no needs."

I can recall two professors with whom I connected on this subject. They realized my life had been shaped by the death of my father and my effort to stay connected to him until the very end; they understood and wanted to influence change. They encouraged me to expand my knowledge and learn what it takes to be present to patients and families as they grieved. They insisted that I become an agent of change, someone who would foster the need for touch and intimacy at any time in the continuum of life and death. To me, this support and acknowledgement felt like a spiritual connection of intimacy with the educators who understood a part of me that was willing to step out of a box and be a voice for others.

Like the above example, an intimate moment may be one in which people take that extra effort to understand you and your passion to make a difference. At the same time, I learned to believe in my capacity to grow beyond the limits ever imagined. This experience enhanced my ability to care for those at the end of life. It also taught me to be ready and willing to support others in their growth despite the risk of controversy.

Dr. Elsie Bandman was my champion. At the time of her death in 2017, her daughter provided these details and remembered all that she was to many of us. Here is an excerpt from her eulogy:

> *Breaking new ground in the 70s, 80s and 90s, Elsie's articles and presentations emphasized the vital role nurses played in the medical experiences of patients and examined moral dilemmas of abortion, euthanasia, and medical intervention, highlighting the importance of including and supporting family involvement. Elsie became the first nurse in New York to be accepted as a Fellow into the American Academy of Nursing.*

Is this not love? Given a strong personal desire to make a difference in people's lives and spending so much of my waking life at work, it became natural for me to seek out individuals who needed additional support to find their way to success. I lived by an intuitive belief that people want to be the best they can be. By supporting the growth and confidence of nurses whom I supervised, I could be increasingly certain that our patients would receive the benefit of their excellent care, which was measurable based on outcomes.

In the world of consulting, where saving time and money was a part of the value system, it became too common an event to find individuals, who were still on a learning curve, being dismissed from their position. I realized that in a perfect work situation, all parties would enter the system having been properly groomed in not only in the work at hand, but in dealing with and communicating with people, from entry level to senior executives. In truth, there is often little time for orientation; this places employees in a situation where they need to act as if they know what they're doing. This can set everyone up for stress and sometimes failure.

Coming from a background where my personal and professional goals always included helping others achieve, as a manager, I devoted time to better understand the members of my team. And almost every time, an employee would return with words of incredible humility when someone cared enough and believed in them when they needed it. No, it wasn't appropriate to provide employees with individual therapy or to replay their family of origin experience, but it was totally acceptable to provide them with a caring relationship. You may need to search far and wide, but there are others in a variety of settings who recognize that we can achieve greater satisfaction and productivity in a culture of understanding, acceptance, and love.

Developing into a healthy adult is that much easier if there are healthy, loving parents and caregivers to model these steps. Coming into yourself and making choices that include love and intimacy is your destiny and your right. You arrive in this world as a loving human being. This love needs to be supported and nurtured. If those around you are incapable of offering this in a consistent manner, you may need to search for ways to find what you need.

This can be accomplished by the people and relationships you elect to surround yourself with. While at work you don't always have influence over who gets hired into the next cubicle or even your selected leadership, but you *do* have control over the friends you choose, who you lean on for support, and those you love. It is especially important to take ownership over those parts of your life that you can control. Determining who you want in your life is within your control.

Your Social Atom

Dr. J.L. Moreno introduced the concept of the Social Atom to assist individuals to visualize the roles other people play in life. This became central to some of the work I performed with therapy groups during my practice in New York. Moreno believed in concepts that stepped away from the original Freudian emphasis of seeing man solely as developing an individual *self* and added a greater emphasis into man and his relationship with others.

Essentially, Moreno reminded us that people need people. He encouraged therapists to explore the conditions perceived using a variety of techniques, including this important survey of the roles in which people engage and their function in aiding others to find success as they proceed through life.

To be more specific, each of us fills a need in each other's lives. For some, it's perceived that many different individuals are necessary to satisfy a sense that life can only be complete with certain relationships present. On a conscious and sometimes unconscious level, we seek out individuals to fill these needs.

For example, what happens when we lose our most valued confidant? Or, what happens when we experience the death of a person who represents our past, someone who understands the challenges we faced without requiring further explanation? Maybe it was a favorite aunt who saw something special in us and was always ready to lend her support. Once again, the better you know yourself, the better you will understand what you need and want from the people closest to you.

The diagram on the following page can be used to showcase your relationships that impact you along your path and create a world around you known as your Social Atom. These are people who are significant yet may not always bring joy. Surrounding yourself with loving people is a choice. This is true for everyone, not just some.

We all focus on the people who provide an opportunity for love and acceptance—your parents, partner, children, siblings, grandchildren, and close friends—however, other people in your Social Atom can include an ex-spouse, who represents a painful loss, or past relationships that once brought you joy, all of which may have been rich in life lessons and still hold some significance in your life.

Perhaps you have not resolved your part in certain relationships and the people are long gone yet you still carry some emotional baggage in your duffle bag of feelings. All of this can weigh you down, making you unavailable to have the energy to start over.

When accounting for all the loving and not-so-loving people in your life, it is acceptable to conclude from now on, "I will only fill my life with loving people." This might be a simple resolution. For example, there is no value in doing business with a dry cleaner who is perceived as disrespectful. Or, you may question doing business with a bank that has consistently terrible customer service. You have a few different options here: You could either choose to say something to the bank manager, try out a new bank, or unnecessarily continue to carry the feelings of rejection around with you.

Starting this process increases your awareness about people around you, by checking in about how the situation makes you feel. With this newly found appreciation, you then take appropriate action.

The Social Atom helps you explore your relationship with people in your life who hold both positive and negative meaning. This includes people with whom you have a strong positive connection with and those who remain significant because of a loss, disagreement, or struggle. This diagram may change each day as you alter those relationships.

Take a moment to consider all the other people who are in your life today. As you place them in the diagram, evaluate the significance they have on you and your life. Show this by the size and location of their circle. What is the current nature of the relationship? Has it changed? Have you lost anyone along the way? Since many people in your life hold a role responsibility that is often reciprocal in nature, determine if you have any "job openings." That is, if you are missing an opportunity for a best friend, how did this happen and what do you need to do to fix it?

An Example of a Social Atom

Use the model of a Social Atom found below to draw one of your own. Always begin by placing "Me" in the center. Feel free to use my model below to guide you. Surround yourself with the people current in your life, others who hold significance from your past, or those roles that are missing and waiting to be filled.

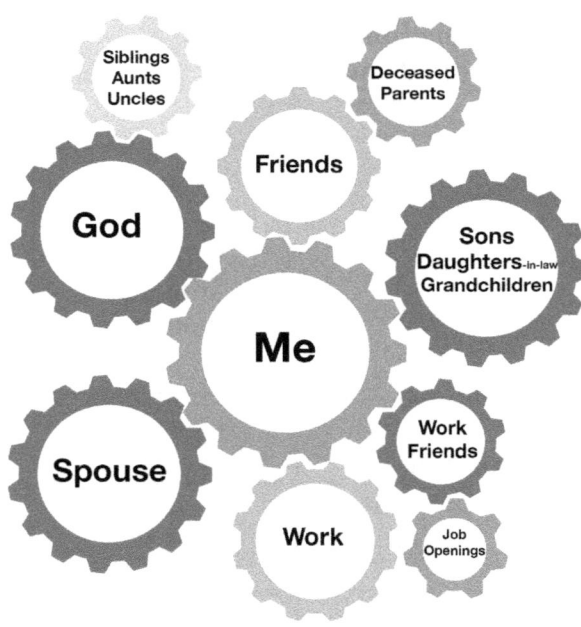

Priorities

In the typical journey of life, you have responsibilities and there will be times when you encounter a need to rearrange some of your priorities in order to meet these responsibilities. Without question, your life continues on until something alters your perspective. For some, it is change emanating from loss, disruption, or death forcing a need for immediate adaptation in order to survive. Intimacy, love, and belonging may take a back seat and seem less important while energy is devoted toward the practical things in life like healing from a devastating illness, paying rent, and having food to eat. Or, you simply recognize, through the course of *individuation*, your needs and wants start to become different from those of your family and more like your contemporaries.

You may have found yourself in the midst of many others who come from various life experiences and traditions that have been fostered and molded for generations. Some of these ways of being may be very attractive. The lesson you discover is that there is more than one way to go through life to find joy. Being open to the differences in people can open your world to many new possibilities.

Loving Yourself

Jim Collins, the author of *Built to Last*, indicates that all corporations have goals and usually select one "Big Hairy Audacious Goal" during their five-year planning to stimulate growth. Loving yourself is one "Big Hairy Audacious Goal" for life. It is probably the most significant part of the equation for greater satisfaction in everything we do as well as finding someone to love. Whatever the circumstances or means that brought you to life thus far, there are no coincidences and no mistakes. Nobody escapes being wounded. Obstacles in life serve as lessons; what matters is what you choose to do with those lessons.

Within every individual there is an abundance of history and stories that make you who you are today. You can choose to constantly remind yourself of a time when someone hurt you and caused you to be bitter; however with strength and courage, life has a way of intruding on the negativity and opening you up to new possibilities.

"Loving yourself requires courage unlike any other. It requires us to believe in and stay loyal to something no one else can see that keeps us in the world—our own self-worth."[23]

—*Mark Nepo*

Early in my adult life, I recognized that while I loved the tenderness and protection I received from my husband, we had other needs. Our children added a joy that lasts to this day. Although working full-time and building our careers, as a couple we were determined to provide our children the very best of what they needed and some of what they wanted.

We knew that despite all the material things available in life at the time, they needed us and we needed them. As a result, we vacationed together and offered time for safe areas of independence and time for connection. We carefully carved out time each day in order to get our children to school, to Taekwondo lessons, soccer games, and the multitude of after-school events. Sometimes, this meant starting my workday at 3 a.m. so that a lesson plan could be completed, or taking the kids to a Latchkey Program, a before-and-after-school setting for children of working parents. Our day typically started at 6:30 a.m. in order for me to get to the hospital in time for rounds by 7 a.m. My husband left on a bus to New York City at 5 a.m., and often didn't return until 6 p.m., but he was "on" and available as soon as he arrived home. We all spent weekends together, with much of Sunday at church. How meaningful it was for each of us to take roles that allowed us to use our time and talents effectively by serving and giving back to God. It was through Him that we became parents to these wonderful children, never once taking them for granted.

This life of giving represented loving and believing in myself and the people around me. It meant forgiving, not always because the person deserved it, but because I needed peace. It meant finding a husband who could tolerate my spinning on a dime when either work or home priorities came to the foreground. It meant being present to our aging parents. And it meant a conscious effort at work to nurture the best in everyone. It meant being aware of the needs of our community and our world. All of this was a challenge, but our primary goals were to be faithful and loving partners and parents and to honor all that we had to give.

But there were still "job openings" in my family's Social Atom. Surely, we needed best friends. In particular, I needed a best girlfriend, someone who shared my thoughts as a woman about developing professionally while raising a family. I also felt my husband and I needed the friendship of other couples who enjoyed some of the things we liked to do.

Over the years, completing my education and moving to new locations for jobs made it difficult to find people who were able to be present to our vigorous schedule. Back then, we were still on the cusp of electronic communication—there were no cell phones, emails, social media, or texts that now enable people to maintain long and meaningful relationships without being in close proximity.

Finding Room for Love and Intimacy in Your Social Atom

Given the strong desire to love and be loved, people generally set out during their teen years or young adult life exploring what this means. While family can be many things to many people, emerging families used to be centered on the model of a heterosexual couple committing to a relationship through marriage. Today, we have a growing number of single parent and blended families.

There are also a number of late Baby Boomers, Millennials, and Gen Zs who altered the norms and added the experience of extended periods of time living together with or without marriage. Some attribute this difference to economic reasons—after all, it is more cost-effective to live in an apartment with more than one person. However, it is also possible that fear of loss or models stemming from the influence of divorce from previous generations has stimulated a strong desire to maintain independence even within the context of a committed relationship.

Women and men are learning to establish boundaries and redefine their roles in the household as each member is likely to be gainfully employed whether working inside or outside of the home. Sharing a home—either for a sexual relationship or the benefit of reducing financial burdens—leads to the redefining of the term *family*.

The acceptance of homosexuality allows the expression of love to a larger group of individuals who choose a lifestyle in a LGBTQ relationship. According to a *Newsweek* article, as of June 26, 2015, all states license and recognize marriage between same-sex couples as a result of the Supreme Court decision in Obergefell v. Hodges, though Mississippi did not honor this legislation until March 2016.[24] Marriage is now a fundamental, legal right for same-sex couples, as is the right to adopt children.

No matter what type of relationship you choose, in selecting a partner, each member needs enough "ego strength" to support themselves and also the "ego strength" of their partner. Freud used the concept of "ego strength" to mean resilience—the ego helps us maintain emotional stability and to cope with both internal and external stress. Just as we focused a great deal on the development of *self* in Chapter 1, couples need to do similar work. In understanding where the engaging qualities of one person intersects with the engaging qualities of the other, it is possible to predict areas of harmony.

When two individuals have qualities, beliefs, opinions, and values that differ significantly, it is more likely they will be in greater discord. How exactly does this happen when most relationships start out with the couple appearing to be so well-aligned? It might be related to the failure to understand and communicate their interests, their values, attitudes, and beliefs that are and always were important to them. At times, the fear of loss stifles openness and honesty early in the relationship, which can lead to a discovery of differences later on.

Loyalty, honesty, dependability, happiness, and open communication are often represented as values in the early relationship and in sustaining a successful relationship in the long term. However, having a successful relationship takes work. The work requires honesty and commitment to communication, negotiation, and a willingness to compromise.

Remember, there are times when we need to give up something in order to get something in return. As time goes on, there may be evidence of a different experience. Perhaps one or both members did not see the other individual as clearly as they thought before living together and sharing responsibilities. Some fail to be faithful to the effort it takes to make a relationship work and even see it easier to start over again. Over time, this action is easily detected in behaviors and words.

Name the Five Engaging Qualities You Seek in an Individual

Let's go back and remind ourselves of the earlier exercise we used to articulate and better understand our own personal qualities and traits. It is equally important to identify those characteristics that are important to you when you invest in a relationship.

Your Engaging Qualities from Chapter 1:

1._____ 4._____
2._____ 5._____
3._____

Now, from the list below, select the five most important qualities you hope to find in others:

1._____ 4._____
2._____ 5._____
3._____

able	energetic	loving	searching
accepting	extroverted	mature	self-assertive
adaptable	friendly	modest	self-assured
aware	giving	nervous	self-conscious
bold	happy	observant	sensible
brave	helpful	organized	sentimental
calm	honest	patient	shy
caring	idealistic	powerful	spontaneous
cheerful	independent	proud	sports-minded
clever	ingenious	quiet	sympathetic
complex	intelligent	reflective	tense
confident	introverted	relaxed	trustworthy
dependable	kind	religious	warm
dignified	knowledgeable	respected	well-mannered
empathetic	logical	responsive	wise
			witty

Prioritize the list and compare it to the engaging qualities you selected in Chapter 1. Are they the same or different? Are you finding that the qualities you maintain as a standard for yourself match the same values and qualities you hope to find in others? This provides a great beginning conversation to explore that which is important to you. If you are currently seeking new relationships, let this be your guide to better define the things you like or even dislike in others.

Particularly important is the level of maturity, accountability, and responsibility each individual accepts in developing and maintaining relationships. When either of the lists demonstrate differences in attitudes, beliefs, or behaviors, a person may choose to flee rather than to do the work needed for a successful relationship. That may not be a bad thing if you are not yet committed to each other. When a person's greater interest is to have a casual encounter or a relationship at all costs, it is possible they may present an image that would be more acceptable than the reality of exactly who they are.

It is also possible for someone to be totally lacking in awareness about the fact that the way they live their life matters and more importantly may have an effect on others. I often hear surprise and disbelief that the person is not actually the way they presented themselves. This occurrence is related to a lack of honesty on the part of one or both members of the couple. One is failing to provide the truth and the other is failing to accept reality.

Of course, other changes may occur that contribute to the demise of a relationship. Not all of us age well and one or both parties may place image above other, more endearing qualities. Or, perhaps one's partner has lost a job and can no longer provide financially. The success or failure of a relationship is usually not isolated to one cause or one situation, but more likely an accumulation of changes in several of the qualities described.

If a crisis occurs on top of already existing tension, an event such as the loss of a child can either strengthen the relationship as the couple finds solace or create irreconcilable alterations to the relationship. The pain of grief may cause distance in the couple's relationship. Instead of supporting each other and finding growth, one or both may discover that the relationship no longer supports them. Loss can also weigh people down to the point of complicated bereavement and depression that changes a person and makes them unapproachable.

Love and Intimacy as We Age

During an early phase of a relationship, couples generally show a great deal of interest in physical contact, including, kissing, touching, and sexual encounters. Many couples look for ways to bring joy to each other. There may be concerted efforts to express love through gifts, cards, flowers, or surprise dinners, all to keep the relationship alive. After some time, there is an unfortunate tendency to take each other for granted. Special glances, expressions of thanks and appreciation along with words of love, may diminish. Sexual prowess during the aging process may reduce or eliminate close contact and stimulation. Instead of addressing this change, members of a relationship may try to ignore or deny what is before them.

When you think back to all those things a person may need to feel loved, respected, and appreciated, this is the time when it is critical to communicate. Love has no limits and can endure just about anything if both parties are clear about the condition in which they find themselves. There are opportunities for adaptation and change that can bring back the joy and intimacy to most relationships.

Ask yourself what you need. Is it to be held or showered with gifts? Is it more expressions of respect and appreciation? Ask yourself what keeps you from verbalizing this. Find a way to enter into a conversation. If you truly love the person, begin your crucial conversation with that fact. Avoid saying "you." Instead use "I" and "we." Then state what you know and ask for support to respect that your needs are valid.

I encourage each of you to determine the engaging qualities you wish to live by and to review what you perceive are the values and beliefs of your partner. Acknowledge the differences and similarities as they exist in the present. Engage in a conversation with the intent that your partner will be interested in repairing your relationship and hopefully willing to engage in some personal growth. Avoid judgement and blame. Remember, it takes two to make or break a relationship.

Also, remember that you are one of the most loving people in the world. You deserve to have people choose to be with you and long to have you in their life. You are a precious soul that merely needs to be dusted off and placed into action. Real love carries no doubt and your partner wants and needs you as much as you need them. Enjoy this part of your journey. It takes work, but it is well worth the investment.

Finding the Words to Say

You have been learning the importance of defining yourself, embracing a set of qualities, and taking responsibility for who you are and who you want to be. You looked into your past, your family of origin, and your own life's events so that you can understand the people and circumstances that have shaped you.

This chapter is meant to broaden your appreciation of human communication. It is a preliminary summary, giving you the basis from which you can gain insight. It supports your growth in learning more about the significance of effective communication (including listening skills), which will allow you a far better chance to be successful in your relationships. Let's agree that communication is important at home, at work, and in all your social interactions.

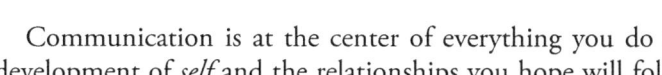

Communication is at the center of everything you do in life, including the development of *self* and the relationships you hope will follow. Communication is not only an exchange of data but, more importantly, it's the way people relate through their use of words, feelings, gestures, and behaviors. It is the way you impress others, or even how you might get passed over, solely by what you say and how you say it.

Communication is a powerful representation of who you are and all that you want to be. It may provide a clue to your level of interest and passion about a subject, your respect and attraction to another individual, your educational preparation, and your use of language to align with your ability to negotiate the world through a keen sense of perception and judgement. Whether buying a car, interviewing for a job, asking for a date, or delivering bad news, communication is the way in which people express their needs, desires, and discontent. It includes information you send and, most significantly, how deeply and effectively you listen.

Communication brings so much joy to people in a relationship when candid displays are used to express love, commitment, and acceptance. Whether at home or at work, people long for the words to be spoken that validate they are doing a good job, that they bring meaning to the life of a relationship, or that they simply matter.

In a love relationship, you may look for the tenderness that can be expressed by a physical demonstration or that loving gaze across a room that is telling the world, "I only have eyes for you." While this seems easy to do, people become complacent and may forget to address simple phrases and behaviors that communicate appreciation for having someone to rely upon for comfort and feedback, whether positive or negative.

People also want and need to be touched from the day of birth until they are very old and even close to the time of death. I firmly believe that the lack of touch and the absence of words conveying love and tenderness creates an emotional void that contributes to a question of value and worth. Psychologists report the term "touch hunger." This is not about sex, which can diminish as you age. Satisfying your touch hunger requires you to have meaningful physical contact with another person. Failing to meet your needs for human touch can have profound emotional, and even physical, consequences.[25]

The most exaggerated example of a loss of connection between people occurs when silence sends a message of disinterest or anger. The lack of contact can critically impact the success of true communication. They say, "silence is deafening" and can have a negative impact on the future of a relationship. It may lead to termination of the relationship and also harm the psyche of people involved.

It takes us back to our previous discussion of the work of Dr. Harry Stack Sullivan, the early developmental theorist, who indicated that children experience either "good me, bad me, or not me" messages from adults.[26] Using silence during the context of a relationship represents detachment and is often perceived as more damaging than being criticized, punished or, perhaps, even being physically harmed. It confirms the "not me" experience that projects a lack of worth and leads to an individual feeling discounted or disregarded.

The impact of silence on children and adults is not always fully understood. Children internalize feelings and behaviors and often hold themselves responsible for other people's conduct. You might find individuals who lived through punishments that included silence later seeking forgiveness and overcompensating through life, just to avoid this potential from happening again. Often the adult using silence as a response, hardly understands the long-term effect.

Silence can be so devastating to a person's ego that it may be just the thing needed to initiate the "fight or flight syndrome," resulting in an individual preparing for battle or fleeing, never to return to the person they were before. These injuries leave a mark and can even damage future relationships when the adult recreates a similar coping method to avoid confrontation. Silence, therefore, represents a loss that may not be able to be repaired.

People use verbal and written communication to influence a change in a situation or mindset. It is also possible to affect others through behaviors that communicate a range of feelings like love, anger, or disinterest. In so doing, communication actually has several important elements to consider.

Elements of Communication

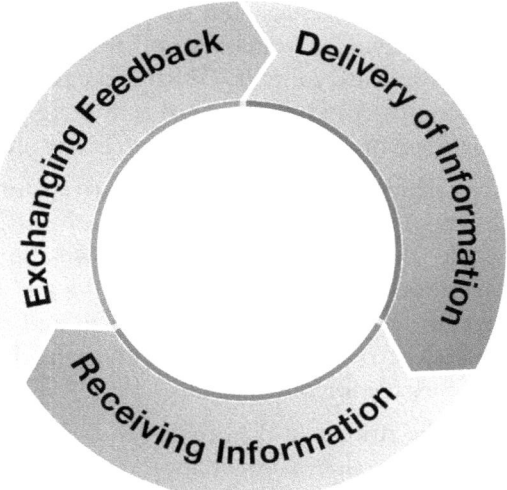

The Feedback Loop

In case you have forgotten the basic elements of communication, it is the process of transferring information so that the message received is the same as the message sent. The sender generally selects a verbal or written mode and prepares what is to be said while controlling the environment to make sure the exchange is successful. The message is sent; feedback is solicited. The feedback is more than the response or agreement with the content sent. It requires a statement of what was heard.

The receiver observes the process, listens, reads, and filters out any distractions. Then the receiver is obligated to provide feedback and encourage the sender to make any necessary adjustments to be sure the message is clear. Then both the sender and receiver prepare to act on the exchange. If you believe this is more complex than you ever considered, you are correct. When people are simply not prepared to do this kind of work, they inevitably struggle with understanding each other and often give up.

As you can see above, communication is quite complex, and it influences the way in which people perceive you. Our thoughts, words, feelings, and actions need to be in sync so that anyone receiving our message emerges with a sense of clarity. When verbal and written communication is poorly aligned with a person's behavior or action, it is possible to perceive this as a "double message." Individuals describe this as receiving mixed signals about the intent of a person's interest in pursuing a relationship.

Essentially, a person's physical response such as a smile or gesture may not match a feeling response or the words being said. It then leads to a sense of confusion over the actual meaning of the message and the best response to provide. Be a careful observer to this behavior in yourself or others and correct it by seeking clarification. You may have to ask yourself, "What is the real meaning and intent behind my communication?" An important goal is to bring people together, not deter them by sending them on a wild goose hunt to better understand.

Just as important in achieving and facilitating effective communication is the need to hear and listen. At times, it is only through the offhanded benefit of losing one's hearing, do you find couples turning down the sound of the TV so they can be less frustrated by mistaking what is being said and what is being heard. With hearing aids, telephones, cell phones, texts, and social media, there are few external physical barriers or obstacles standing in the way to effective communication and no excuse for why it occurs.

The only exception is the attitude of the people involved. Communication once again is based on what a person values as important at that moment in time. Is it more important to be able to follow the last football play or to listen to your significant other? In either case, the communication, or lack thereof, sends a message.

For some, communication provides an experience of joy and an outlet to a stressful day. All of us know at least one person who has the gift of gab. My mother-in-law, who was normally quiet and reserved yet had a wonderful twinkle of joy, looked forward to a gathering of her friends each month. We called it a meeting of the "shady ladies" as they used this time to vent about their everyday life circumstances. Interestingly the ladies observed the same policies one may find in a corporate confidentiality clause. Their policy? "What happened in Bayside, stayed in Bayside."

For others, the thought of addressing someone on the phone or presenting a case where we believe something is unfair creates a great deal of stress. We still find people responding like a deer in headlights or shrinking away from direct confrontation of even the most carefully and strategically designed exchanges of information. Aside from having the ability to communicate in a variety of ways, we continue to find psychological impediments to the degree that people consistently report trouble talking to their partners, children, or co-workers. Talking "to" may be one of the considerations. But what seems to get in the way are psychological causes along with poor speaking and listening habits that may have existed over time.

The psychological factors include a person's sense of fear or intimidation about the nature of the discussion. It may also be a by-product of poor self-esteem or uncertainty about decisions that may have led to unwanted consequences. The roles people play, our own internal communication, and the influence this has over each of us become important factors.

Fritz Perls, the founder of Gestalt therapy, created a concept known as Top Dog/Underdog to demonstrate an example of our internal dialogue. Essentially, when an inner conflict of two opposing forces appears, our intention is to resolve the issue. This could represent situations such as:

- Meeting your own needs vs. pleasing other people
- Holding down a secure job vs. doing the work you love to do
- Wanting to express your differences vs. fear of conflict and rejection

These internal dialogues go back and forth several times—sometimes over a period of time—until a decision is made or the needs are denied. Dr. James Yates, a Gestalt psychologist, suggests we need the role of a "Watchdog." It is possible to provide this as yet another internal voice, but likely you will need a facilitator.[27] Frequently the Watchdog may ask:

- What are your thoughts and beliefs about the issue?
- Can you describe the emotions that you feel when thinking about this?
- What do you want or need from each side of the argument?
- What do you want from your Watchdog?

I am convinced that couples experiencing infidelity allow the behavior to go on longer than necessary because of fear and uncertainty. Their silence on the subject buys them time. The truth can often be painful, but most definitely stimulates a need to address required changes, ranging from mutual appeals to ultimatums that could end the relationship. Denial can set in and eliminate the important step of addressing the fact that something has gone wrong.

As a therapist, I find one or the other partner eventually gathering the courage to ask outright: "Are you seeing someone else or have you simply fallen out of love?" While the response may be direct and honest, I would be a wealthy woman if I had a dollar every time an unfaithful individual not only denied the presence of another person in their life, but also reacted angrily to the query. The suspicious spouse then seeks out ways to validate their belief or goes on thinking they are being paranoid. Neither is an enjoyable journey.

Today, communication makes and breaks billion-dollar deals and romances. We live in a world where people text invitations and set up plans to meet for social and business matters. The sooner you address any differences or disappointments, the sooner you will have an opportunity to resolve them without taking drastic steps amounting to total loss. This communication works best when, not only meeting it head on, but with all parties in the same room.

Remember, it is not only what we say, but how we say it, as well as all of those non-verbal messages that come along the way. The goal is to reduce misunderstanding. Being accountable means doing all within your power to be understood. Sadly, some people choose to use text messaging to end a relationship or even a marriage. This activity demonstrates avoidance, a coping measure that takes the place of direct communication.

In reality, communication hasn't truly occurred unless someone has sent out thoughts and feelings in an exchange that allows an understanding of the message and a return of feedback. The message indicating "It's not you, it's me" hardly allows the receiver a chance to fully understand what just happened to them. Instead, it is an occurrence similar to a hit and run.

It may be hard for us to admit, but a great deal of communication occurs in our heads. There is a continuous flow of what you see and hear as you interpret everything based upon physical and psychological responses. If that isn't enough, attach a catalog of historical events, rich in emotions, that may prejudice the information occurring before you. Each of us tends to pre-judge every situation; it's in our nature to want to be successful in every encounter with another person. For instance, in a work situation, if we are invited to participate in a planning meeting, several types of communication are occurring simultaneously. We may be pleased to be included while also feeling anxious about our ability to provide information effectively. In the end, we want to impress others with our knowledge and judgement.

If you are facing a social or intimate relationship encounter, there are opportunities for a joyful experience as well as a potential for fear. Some people are flooded with old messages of "not good enough" or "not worthy" or "not on the same level" as another individual. This simple reality takes us right back to the work each of us needs to do prior to opening the door to a relationship. As previously stated, it's vital to have a positive regard for yourself and a belief that your interaction with another individual will positively add to both of your experiences.

Chapter 6: Finding the Words to Say

Yes, everybody needs somebody, and likely, after completing your Social Atom exercise in Chapter 5 you will learn that you need more people than you realize. They may include your housekeeper, your mechanic, your doctor and dentist, your parents, teachers, minister or rabbi, and all the people you identify as within that special circle of loving you and being loved by you. The ways in which people serve you and provide meaning to your life is remarkable. It is worthy of your gratitude.

In fact, in the southern United States, you may hear a person end a verbal exchange with, "I appreciate you." This expression is meaningful for the sender and the receiver who usually stops and acknowledges that they have been positively touched. The lesson is that you matter and have the capacity to spread kindness in such simple, yet meaningful ways.

No one is immune to having a failed committed relationship or suffer from being misunderstood or rejected for who you are. With all the opportunities to live each day modeling kindness and love, it may come as a surprise that another person may see you differently than how you see yourself. When this occurs, it is possible that there is something within the way you communicate that is in disrepair. Communication can be the culprit if we are ineffective in the way we speak our truth or if we totally fail to communicate our thoughts and feelings.

Managing Conflict

It's safe to say that much of what we communicate is based upon our own well-developed filter, monitored constantly by our perceptions about people and life. What you perceive is a complex process influenced by messages from the past, the person you have become, and how you are feeling at the time of an exchange. Our perception then becomes our reality. It is also influenced by the way you interpret what you see in people and the judgement you have about their function or worth.

I refer you to a favorite example of people and their perceptions that's found in a TV show involving a corporate CEO arriving at the workplace presenting himself as a new employee ready to learn. "Undercover Boss" intends to capture a true vision of the people working for him so that he can learn their attitudes and beliefs about their company's mission and values. The underlying premise is that at times people avoid direct, honest, and open communication even when it may enhance their success at work. Through this process, he gains the ability to assess how well the employees accept change. Many of the front-line employees are kind and welcoming, but there are those who have no intention of accepting this new employee. Not only are they unhelpful, but critical and see no hope that training this person will make a difference. The employee's attitude remains until it is discovered that the orientee is actually the one who signs his weekly paycheck.

This is a humbling experience from which we all can learn. It raises concerns about people in the workplace: Do you behave differently toward a person who is considered important? Or, did you learn, as I did, to treat everyone with the same amount of respect?

Life presents us with a variety of people, some willing to be accountable and responsible and ready to engage in relationships while others are constantly on guard waiting for the worst in people. Both types are based on learned behavioral responses, often having to do with past experiences.

At work, old hurts and rejections tend to make people vigilant to the possibility that people in their workplace may cause them to lose their status or place in the pecking order. When you find yourself encountering a person who seems angry and on guard, it is common to ask yourself, "What did I do or didn't do to create this hostility?"

As you become certain about who you are as an individual, it will become quite clear that you may not have a dog in this fight. You will become better able to manage the anger being projected toward you without needing to own it.

When facing interpersonal conflicts, a generally uncomfortable experience, wisdom tells us to protect ourselves. Perhaps you represent someone from the individual's past, or the nature of your relationship replays past experiences. While you may want to dismiss this occurrence and head for the hills, I encourage you to take a more careful look at what is being said or what you are being accused of.

Examine the possibilities and take responsibility for that which is yours. In particular, pay attention to your reaction when, seemingly without cause, you become the center of someone's wrath. Has this happened to you before? If so, you may want to note similarities as it may represent information that has been hidden to you. This is indicated in the Johari Window, a tool that was created to allow people to communicate and ultimately 'open up' and improve awareness of each other.[28]

This is not always easy and is dependent upon the nature and extent of your relationship with the person. As a course of action—and to remain intact yourself—imagine you're a window screen. Take in what is being said, but let it quickly leave you. This will allow you to review the occurrence, yet not become overwhelmed. Again, consider who or what you represent to the person.

Conflict tends to raise a variety of issues from the past with evidence of old wounds or unresolved grief. Is there something about this relationship or the pattern of new losses that touches some pain in the individual to the point that they need to lash out? What does this occurrence feel like? Are you becoming anxious or guarded? Where do you feel those feelings?

Managing conflict of this nature is an ideal next step, but it requires fortitude. Is the issue worth the effort it will take to resolve it, or do you imagine it will pass with time? Is the person significant to your everyday life? Do you need to enlist validation and support?

Christa,[29] a therapy client, reported that over a three-year period, episodes of anger and rage were directed toward her by a colleague on two distinct occasions. She was troubled by the experiences and brought it to her therapy session, describing it as so "out of character for her relationships with other colleagues at work."

Christa was viewed as having considerable insight into the work at hand and often shared what she learned so others could experience the same success. In reconstructing the situation, it became clear that the individual with whom she had the conflict was struggling to maintain her position. In both instances, Christa's colleague was being questioned about her approach to work and was experiencing a loss of confidence and mounting insecurity in the ability to be accepted by her supervisors. There had been talk of layoffs and she was not seen as having a positive influence over the work environment. This colleague speculated that Christa's presence represented a potential threat because she brought more value to the team, was well-liked, and appeared to have more job security.

Christa bravely approached the other employee to try to better understand her perspective, hoping this last attempt would be helpful. When this failed to alleviate the tension, Christa enlisted her supervisor and requested a joint meeting. The employee was actually identified previously by another supervisor as being disruptive. Since this same employee's behavior had created issues before, this situation turned into a personnel matter resulting in the employee being terminated.

The incident raised Christa's concern as she viewed herself as a team player, someone who wanted everyone to be successful. In particular, she felt misunderstood and began to question herself. Her supervisor supported her and encouraged her to move on, but to ask herself if there was something to be learned. This entire incident became a lesson reinforcing the need to be accountable and responsible for herself and to honor boundaries.

Can you identify with Christa and her actions? Have you had any situations at work that need to be addressed and better understood from the perspective of learning more about yourself? How do you proceed through your life at work? Are there any troubling conflicts that impact your level of comfort? How do you manage these professionally? Take a moment to write down your answers to these questions in the space provided on the next page.

_____
_____
_____
_____
_____
_____
_____
_____
_____
_____

Impressions and Perceptions

Any one of us can be guilty of judging others prematurely. Before meeting someone for the first time, you may even consider who they are and what they represent. Growing up, I used to hear, "All Catholic school girls are wild. They have to live under the nun's rules all day and they go crazy when school lets out." This was very far from the truth. But perceptions can be problematic when the roles people play are the target of absolute statements.

While people generally present themselves as true to who they are, they can also be a fabrication of who you want them to be. To avoid loneliness, people sometimes make compromises and invite people into their lives merely to fill a void. As a result, conversations may be directed to receive only the answers you want to hear. However, if you are diligent in identifying the engaging qualities that are important to you in a person with whom you form a serious relationship, you will be better able to hone in and explore these characteristics early in your communication.

This is the time to be honest with yourself. To be clear, if you describe yourself as industrious, hardworking, and interested in being a high achiever, you will want to be cautious before taking into consideration others who may have qualities that are inconsistent with this way of life. At the very least, your partner needs to be tolerant of the *you* you are becoming. If someone enters your life creating an instant excitement and interest, how do you manage learning that they haven't worked in three years and are homeless? Does this raise any conflict between your values and your desires? Or, are you inclined to try to "fix" the person and make it all better?

It may be an exaggeration, but I offer this example because I want to stir your thinking. Sometimes a relationship fails merely because you are not the right match. It is far better to learn this early in the relationship rather than waiting five years only to learn that your much dreamed about partner simply doesn't have the same goals and desires you have about your choices in life. At these moments, step outside of yourself long enough to hear the voice of your best friend. What would they tell you? Better yet, be that best friend and listen to your own heart.

At the beginning of a relationship, the information each of you communicate about yourselves is generally the start of a belief system. Given everything is equal and you both are operating from an honest place, you want and need to believe that which is being told to you. In a similar manner, you will want to provide information about yourself that is clear and honest while avoiding information that might discredit you from the start.

You likely have heard the adage, "loose lips sink ships." This statement was used on World War II posters discouraging people in the military from conversation about the war effort. It implies that each of us holds the responsibility in controlling how information is perceived, received, and used, often for the outcome we hope to achieve. It makes sense that, during your first encounter with someone, you likely won't be getting on a ladder to access your box full of secrets that sits atop your closet shelf, tightly sealed and bound with pink ribbons.

That box may contain parts of your life that you are not ready to share, and at times, information never to be shared. In fact, it would be questionable for you to share intimate information at this early stage of getting to know someone. When meeting for the first time, it's wise to engage in safe talk and share information that anyone might find out about you on Facebook, Twitter, or LinkedIn. After all, our goal as humans is to impress and encourage a return visit.

Openness is a wonderful virtue, but it can be used with some discrimination to protect information not ready for public consumption. Openness is how much you choose to share at a given time. However, honesty is an important quality that needs to be a part of all relationships. It allows complete trustworthiness and reliability on all that you or others communicate with you. If you look back at those failed committed relationships, my guess is that one or both of the parties did not exercise this level of responsibility. Honesty is a virtue that becomes easier with practice and needs to be a regular everyday experience.

Honesty needs to be established early in a relationship, along with the many other values you have learned and captured by doing the exercises in this book. The more skilled you are in your ability to communicate—including an awareness of what is being said, the feelings behind them, and the behaviors present—the better you will maintain control over your environment, including the people you choose to have in your life and those who choose to remain with you.

You will discover a world where there is reciprocity in maintaining the value of honesty. This includes an expectation that others will also hold this behavior in high regard. If you are living a life that is completely honest and open, your goal is always to reduce ambiguity and to enable others to succeed alongside you.

If you are being honest, you need to be willing to state exactly what is important to you. You may need to remind yourself what is desired, topics that are off limits, and those that you may choose to communicate as the relationship progresses and trust is developed. For example, have you established standards about who you date and the way you would like a relationship to proceed? Are you comfortable putting your thoughts and feelings into words? Is engaging in sex early in the relationship the message you want to send?

If you recall, all behavior has meaning. Be sure that the message you send is the message you intend to send. It can be interpreted that sexual behavior is a response to casually liking someone when, in fact, you would prefer this act to come at a different time in your relationship. Imagine finding the other person very appealing, but also having this value getting in the way of your taking action. Your honest communication about the subject of engaging in sex is significant. Tell your partner the whole of what you are thinking and feeling. Once again, it is all about knowing yourself, what you need and want, and then being able to verbalize your wishes or use communication in such a way that another person can be clearer about expectations.

When I was in my last years of college, I shared an apartment with a roommate who was in a social status above mine. I was the constantly poor, constantly studying or working, rather naïve individual just trying to get by. I recall Rhonda proudly informing me that her mother had arranged dates for her with "suitable" possibilities. It was quite the event as mother and daughter would be picked up by their chauffeur to be driven to Lord & Taylor or Bergdorf Goodman to buy a "suitable" outfit for the "suitable" date.

One day she came home with a full-length fur coat. I remember thinking to myself what a threat that might be to most people in our age group who cared to take her out. She would often return after the date to announce, "He took me out nicely." I imagined that was code for "a lot of money was spent on dinner." Sadly, the men in question hardly ever returned for a second "suitable" date.

Putting up walls and covering up with a variety of masks, like a fur coat, becomes a full-time job. It means you have to take careful notes about what you communicate about yourself and to whom. The more pretense you create hoping to be accepted, the greater the risk you place in losing your own reality.[30]

People can end up living a lie to the degree that they are unsure what is real and what is not. A person may want to have a certain lifestyle, but may not have all the pieces in place to be successful. Perhaps they dropped out of school and never completed that accounting class or their degree. Yet, they proudly display a Bachelor's degree in Business as part of their resume. The saddest part of all is that people see through this process and view the individual as a liability needing to be removed. Also, the individual found to be dishonest runs a risk of attracting people who are also questionable in their values and actions.

Putting What You Learn into Action

The work you are addressing in this book encourages you to take an active role, no longer waiting for someone else to validate you or to tell you what to think and feel. I encourage you to look within and start to find your strength. Consider your life experiences and all that you have learned. Are there situations and conflicts that are more easily resolved than others? Are you struggling with certain aspects of your life while another part is bringing great reward and confidence?

This is your opportunity to own the part of you where you have gained skills and proficiency about how to proceed through life. Give yourself credit for all your successes as you will build upon them and remind yourself especially when you might be feeling down. Learning more about yourself and how best to verbalize your opinions and beliefs allows you to operate from a position of strength. However, it takes training to know how to do this effectively. Much like corporations offering annual review classes on the subjects of ethics or crisis intervention, having this skill about common sense situations in life prepares you to communicate spontaneously and, thereby, meet your needs as well as honor the needs of others.

This work is yet another step in your preparation to engage in this sometimes-uncertain world we live in. It is important to name any thoughts you may have about your life and the feelings attached to them. You might even have times of loss yet to grieve. Take the time to do so. Then, you can skillfully integrate your experience and what you know as your own truth.

By now, you are learning what is yours and sorting out values and opinions you may have learned along the way. It is time to discard anything that you learned that may no longer serve a purpose toward your growth. Your family likely had considerable influence on your overall success. Honor their willingness to be present and recognize that even in times when there were differences and challenges, people from your past contributed to your learning important life skills. As you proceed on your path, you will gain an ability to act from a posture of wholeness.

Facing Conflicts

When facing a conflict, people tend to test out premises that support their position, hoping to be correct before uttering a word. Human behavior is such that out of fear of loss or rejection, people sometimes take desperate actions. You may recall this concept from our earlier discussion about the Johari Window that states that each of us has a hidden area—those parts of our thoughts and feelings that we keep hidden from others.[31] Perhaps you have created barriers to protect yourself from the experience of an old hurt, even promising yourself you would never let it happen again. However, a protective barrier works both to keep people and things out and to confine us to a life void of future relationships.

As hurt as you may have been, it is possible to resolve the feelings of loss and start again, since human beings instinctively want someone to share their love. This is your moment to better understand how you got here and to determine whether any old behaviors and defenses need to be left behind. As important as it is to protect yourself from being hurt, let that hurt be your teacher as you learn more about yourself and others with the understanding that each new relationship allows you to make better choices.

If you have lived through infidelity, trust will likely be added to the list of necessary requirements in all future relationships. It will be important to communicate this need early on. Do your careful analysis and speak about the importance of this quality and perhaps some of the feelings left over when someone violated your trust. Don't allow someone to convince you ever again that the signs you are seeing are "all in your head." Your perceptions are a way of understanding and interpreting your experiences in life. They don't always align with another person's reality of the same situation and will definitely be a cause for considerable communication.

People might fail us and we might fail ourselves, however, I caution you to be fair in your judgement if you choose to base every relationship on the past one. It takes work to develop the loving, confident person you want to be. When you find yourself, you can more easily reach out and find your counterpart. They are out there looking for you. There is a sense of hope in knowing that all over the world people basically want the same things. People want to feel safe and secure; they want to be accepted for who they are and to gain a sense of belonging. They want to be respected by a special person who not only gives support but will move mountains to help those they care about.

You are likely better able to understand the complexity of situations you will face when reviewing elements of communication. An important takeaway is to learn that it is not about who you should be, but the world of possibilities that bring you the most joy and gratification when being your authentic *self*. People can be hindered in their communication because they are actively intent in trying to prove themselves to others rather than being themselves. Be true to yourself and stop "should-ing."

An Eleventh Commandment could be, "Thou Shalt Not *Should* on Thyself."

Begin by identifying common experiences in your life that may be impacted by honest and open communication. Are you still ruminating about a relationship from your past? Are you wishing for another opportunity to relive the situation or at least be better prepared with what you have to say? Is there really more to learn or is this a lesson of letting go?

Frequent thoughts and feelings:
_____
_____
_____
_____
_____
_____
_____
_____
_____

What keeps me up at night?
_____
_____
_____
_____
_____
_____
_____
_____

What actions do I take or need to take to resolve these concerns?
_____
_____
_____
_____
_____
_____
_____
_____

Engaging in Crucial Conversations

So, what in the world does all this mean? Imagine yourself about to engage in an important discussion, one that may impact your family, your life, or your work. It becomes critical to be prepared for the outcome before you begin. At certain times, all parties anticipate controversy and an output of emotional energy. These events are defined as *Crucial Conversations*, occurring between two or more people where "stakes are high, opinions vary, and emotions run strong."[32]

This is often considered the most difficult of all communication and may have been prevented before it reached this level of controversy. When we fail to engage in a crucial conversation, every aspect of our lives can be affected, from our careers, to our personal lives, and even our health.

After many years of personal work in improving the manner in which I communicate and manage crucial conversations, I was faced with one of my greatest challenges: Being at the bedside of my dying mother. My husband and I, along with our two sons, had cared for her for almost 18 years. Now we faced letting her go. We were all clear about our understanding of death and had the benefit of time and honesty in our relationship with my mother. We had made the effort to have many conversations about her dying wishes. We had the joy of spending time with her during some of her best moments, before her aging created the inevitable and we began to witness a failing of mind, body, and spirit.

In fact, during one quiet moment, she asked me why God chose to keep her on earth for 94 years when He took my dad at age 59. I admitted that I'd never figured out why life happens this way. I hugged her and promised her she would not be alone when her time came. She seemed satisfied with this. But, as was normal in our relationship, we tried to find humor to cope. She added that her sight was poor, she couldn't hear, her mobility was compromised, and she was not so sure her mind was working well anymore. I realized my mother was telling me she was ready to die. I squeezed her tightly and said, "Well Mom, if you were a horse, I would shoot you." She looked up at me and we laughed and cried together because we both knew neither of us had any control.

This conversation became the cornerstone of my being there for her when her time did come. I was incredibly grateful that we had this conversation before the situation was critical. Both my mother and my family were prepared to accept her wishes. However, other family members had avoided this exchange. It brought up the awareness of potential loss and they chose to step away from any conversation like this.

Several months later, when my mother's doctors alerted me that she had developed sepsis and had little time to live, we prepared for her death. Yet, the potential for death still came as a surprise to my siblings. It was frustrating that this discussion had not occurred sooner, but once again we orchestrated a meeting with the hospice physician so they could be part of the decision-making.

This final conversation allowed her to die in peace just three days later. It also allowed those of us present to focus on our grieving, rather than trying to resolve years of regret from other family members. My authentic *self* wanted to honor my mother's wishes, allow each family member to experience their own grief, and to be present to my husband and children who surrounded her at her bed with the love she so deserved.

You may be saying to yourself that nothing of that level of urgency has happened to you. Perhaps you don't think it applies to you. However, if you interact with others long enough and find that living in relationship truly matters to you, crucial conversations will suddenly be seen as essential. My hypothesis is that people tend to avoid issues that are painful or uncomfortable or that may provoke disagreement. In situations with family, people avoid communication that they imagine may be confrontational. There is a tendency to rationalize avoiding action or even engaging in communication. In truth, avoidance then creates additional anger and disruption of the family.

It is quite possible to take more control over situations that impact your life. You might have been convincing yourself that you have no control over your own destiny. In truth, avoidance is a well-known coping mechanism and it is a powerful way to control or manipulate the direction of a relationship. Unfortunately, this behavior then contributes to the burden of the relationship by adding baggage to all involved. As you recognize the value of learning as much as you can about being an effective communicator, consider becoming an ace at this task as well. Try the following steps.

Taking Steps to Be an Ace:

- Evaluate your early life experience in direct and meaningful communication.
- Consider the patterns of communication you learned at home and during professional development.
- Assess the environment in which you find yourself. You may need to teach models of open and direct communication.
- Most importantly, determine your willingness to take risks. Think through the possibilities of the reactions you may receive.
- Be diligent in creating communication that honors others and their perceptions.
- Preface your communication with what you know: For example, "This may be hard for you to hear, but…"
- Recognize that your willingness to engage in crucial conversations may reframe even the most difficult situation.

Instances where we fail to engage in crucial conversations challenge all of us throughout life. A rushed decision can lead to conclusions that shape your reactions and behaviors. This can then cause unexpected consequences. However, information is missing that can help you with your decision.

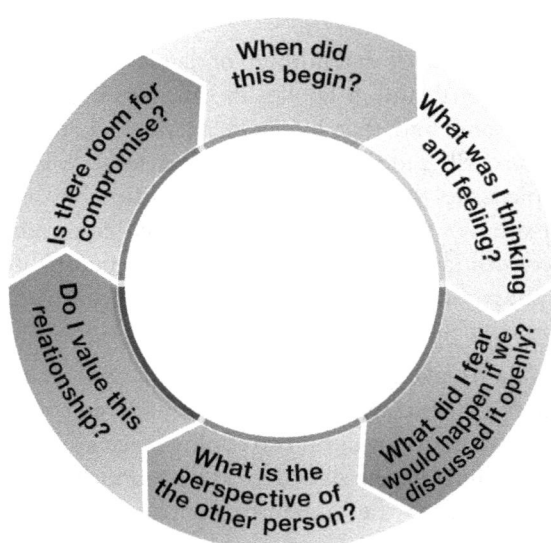

Chapter 6: Finding the Words to Say

How can engaging in communication before reaching a conclusion and taking action assist you?

_____
_____
_____
_____
_____
_____
_____

Communicating from a Value-Driven Approach

It becomes essential to put all of yourself into your communication. You likely have heard people state, "Say what you mean, and mean what you say." Essentially this is another reminder to know yourself well enough to be able to stand behind everything you communicate. The world is relying on your integrity.

As a precursor to effective communication, once again you will need to turn to your engaging qualities. Do you demonstrate honesty? Have you learned to understand your own needs and the needs of others? Have you learned to accept that each person has a perspective about their truth? Can you accept differences among people and, most of all, display authenticity in all you do?

Select a real-life problem or situation that is present to you at this time. Perhaps you have a conflict you are facing at work or at home. Rather than encouraging you to look outward to find a culprit to blame, I challenge you to look inward at the person you have become. In fact, going forward, I am discouraging blame as a solution and instead inviting you to do a cognitive shift by changing your ability to communicate, giving you access to a new perspective about the same problem.

Name your problem:

_____
_____
_____
_____
_____
_____
_____

Taking the position of examining the other person's perspective encourages you to look at all sides of an interaction or a relationship. Ask yourself, "Who ultimately is responsible for the way I'm feeling? What part of this is mine? Have I created a series of crises by avoiding the pain I was feeling because I was afraid to face conflict in the relationship? Did avoidance help to prepare what needed to be said or done? Or did avoidance merely support my denial that the situation needed attention?

Hurt and disappointment can do this to you. It leaves a scar that can make you doubt yourself and forget to feel the memory and glimmer of happiness. You might find yourself *acting out* at others who don't deserve the blame. This only alienates you even further. Or, you may even *act in* with risky behaviors or coping measures that only make it much more difficult to find your way. These behaviors may then define you and complicate life as people outside of you are only seeing the obstructed vision of a human being. The work at hand is then to calm the spirit enough to allow the beauty of your personal *self* to be the first thing someone sees.

Behaviors Exhibited When *Acting Out*:
- Avoiding communication
- Engaging in arguments
- Projecting blame
- Distorting truths
- Exhibiting antisocial behaviors
- Overspending

Behaviors Exhibited When *Acting In*:
- Self-harm
- Explosive behaviors
- Withdrawal
- Depression
- Addiction

Important Factors to Take Away as You Find the Words to Say

Most episodes of communication are successful when individuals have prepared and know ahead of time that which they hope to accomplish as an outcome. If you perceive you are about to be confronted, preface your contact with anything you know to be true. For example, "I'm aware that you have a reluctance to talk about this. I can respect any feelings you may have, but I think we have reached a place where we need to be open and honest with each other."

The ability to communicate your thoughts and feelings is an essential factor in providing others a clear view of your authentic *self,* the one you always want others to know and appreciate. You have so much to offer. Your opinion and the way you perceive the world matters to the whole of all of us. Those people who have the courage to express a different perspective or solution enrich relationships by allowing everyone involved to consider many perspectives about the same situation.

We are so fortunate to have the freedom to think for ourselves and to influence a world that is not always willing to recognize that each person on this earth has something to contribute. Begin with you. Know what you believe is important. Learn to be an effective listener as well as a communicator who welcomes other's thoughts with a willingness to provide their feedback. Without this, communication does not occur and we lose the opportunity to learn.

7

On Grieving

With considerable humility, as I began to write this most important chapter, I offered a prayer. For years during my career, I started each day of work in my office or in the hospital calling upon God to fill me with His wisdom, courage, and strength. There were so many times when clients would present their struggles and I wondered, in all of my humanity, whether I safely managed their pain and helped them regain a sense of control and balance. This time, I asked for wisdom to adequately articulate the information before us so that I can effectively bring you all to a place of peace, to help validate you, and hopefully be your teacher and advocate.

In my years as a nurse and grief therapist, I learned that relationships that developed as I engaged with a person in need always created a sacred place. It was never enough for me to attend all the classes and lectures and to have embraced the latest theories on grief and loss. All of this I did to be sure my foundation remained credible, yet I quickly learned that there was an intimate space, one to be honored, when someone invites you in to be present to their deep, unrelenting pain and fear.

This profound connection allows for two souls to touch, to the degree that the person who is grieving or anticipating grief begins to shed their defenses and starts to believe that someone finally understands. As the therapist, I needed to maintain the courage to allow others to express the whole of their thoughts and feelings without judgement or any effort to control the situation. It is always important to be able to say what you think and feel with someone who understands this pain and allows you to feel it. If this has not occurred in your life, it is your time to do so now.

In our work throughout this book, you labored diligently to reach a better understanding of yourself. You learned about the many qualities you possess that are so endearing and enable you to find success in your personal and professional life. You are working toward a sense of freedom in no longer waiting for someone else to define you as being good enough. However, all the while, you intuitively know something is not quite right in your world. You may have searched for this particular book and this exact chapter after finally acknowledging the reality of a loss, a realization of a disappointment, a regret, or an accumulation of grief.

It is my hope that this book will assist in improving your self-awareness as you search for answers. This chapter is meant to support you wherever you are in the health-illness spectrum. The experience of loss of any kind may temporarily weaken you and make you question your ability to accept all that is happening to you. You may even doubt your ability to get to the other side of your grief. As your Paraclete, your mentor and guide, I am here to remind you of your worth and the strength you have within.

The Crisis of Loss

I was busy at work on a Sunday night during the last phase of a project at Cedars Sinai Medical Center in Los Angeles. This was the climax to years of preparation, in which I had spent every week traveling from my home to California. It was 9 p.m. pacific time when a call came from my husband telling me that our son and daughter-in-law were in a serious car accident in North Carolina. I held my breath as I was certain he was about to tell me they had both died. I learned that a tractor trailer speeding at 70 miles per hour careened into the back of 10 cars on the interstate near our home.

To this day, I am not sure what I said. All I can recall is becoming immediately disorganized and confused. He told me Christopher was injured, but alive. Amber arrested three times at the scene and was airlifted to the tertiary hospital in Asheville where they had a trauma ICU. My mind was whirling trying to find order that would help me make the next step.

I was committed to a serious part of a project and needed to reach out to administrators for guidance. Julie remained calm and made my decision for me. We were staying at the Beverly Hilton. She told me to get a reservation on the next flight out of LAX, check out of the hotel, and leave my rental car keys with the concierge. She would return it the next day. She advised I take a taxi to the airport and go quickly as the last flight of the night would soon be leaving. I realized then how much I needed someone to design my every move, as the news had created an incredible fear of loss leaving a normally capable person unable to problem-solve.

I missed the connection to Atlanta and had to take a flight to New Orleans, then Atlanta, and finally Asheville, which meant I wouldn't arrive until the afternoon the next day. I cried non-stop the entire trip home with my thoughts turning to what I might find. Upon arrival at the hospital, my husband held me as though we both might break. Christopher had multiple fractures and a punctured lung, but he was whole and alive. I knew his most painful injury was the potential loss of his beautiful 26-year-old wife.

Beautiful Amber, full of life with a potential to help others after just completing her Master's degree in Social Work, was removed from life support several days later when it was clear she had no brain activity. I had participated in the process of determining brain function many times as a nurse, but this time it was Amber, Christopher's first love since high school and our first daughter.

This crisis was one none of us had ever experienced and will never forget.

You may be in crisis and, for the first time, realize that you don't have adequate internal resources to deal with the experience of loss. Much like my situation, you may have become immobilized and unclear how to respond. By definition, crises present obstacles to a person's equilibrium when customary efforts to resolve the situation no longer work. It can be a time of danger or opportunity based on the individual response. While we usually think of crises as a sudden traumatic event as is the case with loss, it can be the response to a predictable rite of passage as we proceed through developmental stages of life from adolescence to adulthood and into midlife.

In my therapy practice, my clients usually faced a crisis of loss and often hoped to resolve the tremendous emotional pain experienced by this loss. The pain from loss cannot be measured as one would measure temperature or blood pressure. If anything, it may be related to the amount of love experienced in the relationship, the meaning placed on the lost person, and the awareness of a tremendous void. It didn't matter if the loss was expected or a sudden circumstance. The amount of pain and sorrow was never to be judged. Whether it was the end of the relationship with a friend or spouse, the death of a parent or sibling, the loss of a pet, or a much dreamed about future, the pain of loss is truly in the beholder.

Since I worked with physicians who addressed fertility, it was fairly frequent that clients who were unable to conceive a child were referred to me. They watched others who easily became pregnant, yet this was not the case for them. It often resulted in self-blame and a source of tension and stress for their couple relationship. These clients also verbalized a sense of losing their minds. They were not eating, felt inadequate, and could not function. In these cases, our work was to acknowledge the loss before addressing other ways to manage the issue of infertility. It was a freeing moment when we could redefine all these reactions as grief.

When someone enters a crisis state, they rarely see any options to help them deal with their pain, yet, even in the most critical conditions, there are opportunities to learn how to manage grief. Let me be clear: I don't have a pill or a potion that would eliminate the experience of loss. Loss hardly presents as one size fits all to allow us to consider an easy solution. In truth my use of the word manage is somewhat complicated and faulty in and of itself, as grief is far from an event that can be managed or intellectualized in order to make it go away.

Reaching into the depths of our humanity and oftentimes through the support of others, we need to find a way to cope, something not everyone has in their reserve of life experiences. Without turning to ways to resolve the pain, the experience of loss—the isolation, withdrawal, and a total loss of desire—easily intrudes on the most capable of us. I feel quite certain that the ability to address grief begins with accepting the reality of loss and then being willing to feel the pain.

One way people manage grief, but hardly the optimal choice, is to exercise avoidance. Avoidance is meant to protect you when the reality of loss is unbearable to the degree that it disorganizes a person and places them in a state of shock, denial, and disbelief. Allowing time to make sense of thoughts and emotions may be the only thing that you can do until a more favorable coping measure presents itself. However, avoidance can also cause extreme outcomes when an individual avoids anything related to the issue.

For example, for a woman having trouble conceiving, her grief can make it too difficult to support a best friend at the birth of her baby, resulting in a sense of further social isolation. While that may sound extreme, it does happen. Avoidance—and therefore isolation—is hardly an effective response for loss as humans heal best when they are surrounded by the presence of loving, supportive people.

Stressful life events exist not only in our memories, but in our organs and cells, and research is discovering this connection faster than ever before. Stressful life events causing crisis and grief may be denied and almost buried. In her early teachings, Dr. Candace Pert hypothesized a biochemical link at the cellular level between the mind and the body.[33] This provided scientific evidence to support the work of therapists who described a client's emotional release when performing body work.

I witnessed this when holding joint therapy sessions with a physical therapy colleague trained in craniosacral therapy, or CST. This form of therapy is based on the belief that the musculoskeletal system has influence in maintaining health within our whole body. Apparently, emotional issues can be stored in the soft tissues of the body, bringing about complaints that are physical in nature, yet are most often due to memories rooted in trauma and loss.[34]

At a Gestalt therapy retreat, I remained close to a subject receiving physical therapy in the form of deep massage to the client's kidneys and abdomen. Both of these areas invoked tears as the person remembered something from their past that had been repressed for many years. We supported the person in remembering this memory and revisited it with the support that a psychotherapist could offer. This became a powerful awareness of the connectivity of the whole body.

Chapter 7: On Grieving

It's important to address the fact that physical symptoms can take over and result in a variety of psychophysiological disorders such as high blood pressure, diabetes, and heart disease. This may lead a person to seek help from a primary care practitioner for a variety of symptoms, including headaches, increased heart rate, irritable bowel syndrome, or substance dependencies. If astute, the practitioner will listen with their third ear, a term coined by psychoanalyst Theodor Reik, who discovered the value of listening for a deeper meaning in that which is being said. Hopefully, the practitioner will avoid prescribing anti-anxiety or antidepressant agents unless, of course, grief has lasted to an extent that it is considered by diagnosis as a complicated bereavement disorder.

Complicated bereavement is almost an antithesis to the defining characteristic found with grief. When one is grieving a loss, they experience intense sorrow, numbness, guilt, and anger while working to reach resolution in experiencing a life without the lost person or object. In complicated grief, symptoms escalate over an extended period of time where feelings of loss are the only focus. The individual loses interest in self-care or the needs of others and may even demonstrate prolonged numbness and a desire for isolation. This can be life-threatening and might require further intervention.

Patterns of grief and loss are complicated since they encompass the entire being of an individual—emotional, mental, spiritual, and physical. When grieving, you wonder if the pain and uncertainty will ever end, but previous experience with loss and attempts to resolve the unimaginable pain are directly influenced by an individual's ability to find strength and comfort.

Grief knows no bounds and doesn't adhere to a timetable for when it will be complete. No two people grieve quite the same way, even about the same loss. There are no "right" or "wrong" ways to grieve, although practicing avoidance, especially in saying your last goodbyes, impacts not only you but the dying person as well. This makes it that much more difficult to find models of hope. At the very least, it takes the safety of an accepting environment to allow a person to acknowledge the reality of their loss and then to take the next step to feel their pain.

In October of 2019, I listened to an Episcopal deacon deliver his sermon on the death of a priest; he made it clear that the quiet, gentle man we had just lost had touched many others throughout his service in life. During the sermon, the deacon introduced a poem by Mary Oliver, the late American poet. In her book *Felicity*, she asks three questions in response to the death of her close friend, all of which signify that death has an incredible impact. In her poem, Ms. Oliver indicates some of the challenges of loss—both the physical and emotional struggle in losing someone you love. There is a distinct void when a person who has occupied a significant place or role in your life is now missing.

I recall clients of mine who had lost someone dear to them reporting how frustrating it was to look out at a group of people—in a shopping mall or store or any crowded place—and being certain that they would see their loved one. Or even more difficult, the urge to pick up the phone to share some news and realizing that the person is no longer there.

The instinct when someone is grieving is to take away that pain; too often people are not permitted to grieve. At times, their lack of clarity and unpredictable emotion makes someone else uncomfortable to the degree that a well-intended friend or family member may request a variety of drugs to alter the person's state. In general, this only delays the process of grieving. If emotional absence is too painful, the best one can do is to be present or suggest a referral to a practitioner of grief and loss who is capable of being present to the griever's pain. You may also instinctively and wisely reach out to family and friends who can relate to your experience and guide you to get the proper help you need as you may need more support from a variety of places and people.

There are support groups that address specific kinds of loss such as Compassionate Friends for those dealing with the death of a child, the American Cancer Society through local hospital-affiliated groups in your community, and Centering Corporation, which has hundreds of grief resources. There are also many organizations that support families of children who have died such as Bereaved Parents of the USA, the SIDS network, First Candle, and Share Pregnancy and Infant Loss Support.

The choice of support service may be quite personal and dependent on a person's previous experience with therapists and groups. It may be the rabbi, minister, or priest who was there at the time of death who seems to be the best choice.

Whichever support resources you choose, the important message is that you need not go through your grief alone. When all is said and done, the last piece on a person's agenda is dealing with their grief. It often presents much like a hot stove that, as a child, you learned to avoid.

I witnessed this as a three-year-old as I watched my favorite Aunt Dora being taken from our home by ambulance, never to return. This happened without any adult filling in the important information that she had died and would not be a part of our lives any longer. This was the aunt who carried me to bed each night and prayed over me until I fell asleep. She only spoke Italian but the love she displayed did not need any exchange of words. Her expression was one of love and tenderness as she carefully made the sign of the cross over my forehead as a means of offering spiritual protection through my sleep and beyond.

As an adult, I have to believe that my family was trying to protect me from the pain of loss the night the ambulance arrived. In truth, they likely didn't know how to acknowledge their own loss or communicate loss to a three-year-old, nor were they addressing their own fear of my response, and most certainly didn't realize its significance that would remain with me to this day.

What is Grief and Loss?

Grief and the sadness over loss can be due to your own personal loss resulting from death, loss of a job, a much-wanted life goal, and even a transition over which you have limited control. Or perhaps your grief is not yours at all, but generations of loss which was unresolved and carried on from family member to family member.

We know that grief can account for a person's choices in life. For example, it could date back to wartime when entire families were devastated and killed in unmerciful ways, encouraging later generations to live together in order to secure their protection. This collective grieving even contributed to a sense of survivor's guilt, making it more difficult to accept success in the future.

One of my clients was a child when taken to Auschwitz, a concentration camp in Germany. She lost everyone in her family during the Nazi era when Jewish people and others were exterminated because they did not meet the specifications of a tyrannical leader. She struggled into old age still anticipating and looking for signs that this behavior may exist today and still questioned, "Was there something I could have done to save them?" There was no direct and simple answer to soothe her broken heart, but to remind her of all the many amazing deeds she went on to accomplish in her life.

People who suffered tremendous and meaningful loss that occurred early in their life or in generations before them sometimes remain vigilant to the potential for trauma of loss in the present.

Grief does not limit itself to only actual losses. The *anticipation* of loss can trigger grief, too, and it's enough to stop people in their tracks. Fear of loss and the feelings related to anticipatory grieving represent a deep sadness that resembles the same experience at the actual time of loss. Even the most capable individuals may find themselves changed and dissolved in a set of irrational thoughts and feelings. It may find individuals unable to concentrate on issues in the present as the fear of the sequela of death may overtake them.

Anticipatory grief begins as soon as someone receives a diagnosis of a fatal illness. This is why it is highly encouraged to begin to have open and timely communication among family members. Ask the dying person how they hope to spend the rest of the time they have. It is important to remember that while you may be enveloped by your sense of loss, the dying individual is losing everyone and everything they have known.

When people choose to avoid facing loss, they risk living a life accumulating unresolved grief, which can then become so unmanageable that some people and families become paralyzed with the thought of considering a life worthy of joy. This is where they "opt out" to try to extinguish the pain by using drugs, taking control by suicide, or live a life so consumed with worry about the next potential loss that they foster a self-fulfilling prophesy. These unfortunate souls also lose the opportunity to learn from the previous loss, which means openly addressing their pain.

For some, the fear of loss prevents them from taking the risk to engage in relationships. Imagine a man or woman suffering through the pain of divorce or a failure of an intimate relationship. While the desire for a loving relationship is great, the unresolved experience prevents them from considering a new commitment. Instead of seeing people as having a potential for a loving relationship, the injury creates an angry outer shell that few people are able to penetrate.

As we can see, loss does come in many forms. We grieve the loss of friends, places of comfort, and joyful experiences when we move through the natural progression of one stage of life to another. Think about your teenage *self* as you completed your senior year of high school. By then you likely felt a sense of acceptance and belonging; it can be powerful to be so competent and confident. You were a known entity to your teachers and you carved out your interests. If college was in your plans, you likely prepared all the documents and completed all the required applications to impress the best of admission advisors in the schools of your choice.

For many high schoolers, it's likely that they hardly take time to consider the changes and losses happening during this time in their lives. Some students choose not to say goodbye to their friends and teachers—this is especially the case when young people insist that they'll remain in touch through the advantages of technology. While this may be true, it may also represent avoidance in acknowledging an ending. This not only denies people of the experience of loss, but also denies a person the full acknowledgement of the meaning of change. In truth, during any change or loss, there are feelings of sadness that need to be considered. These experiences offer us our training wheels for facing bigger, more painful losses that may lay ahead.

If it is assumed that taking this next plunge in life is not a favorable step, the emerging adult may not feel secure enough to take the step required in seeking out a new job or a new life in another location. It may very well be related to unresolved loss. In fact, in graduating and leaving school, we are not only leaving

Chapter 7: On Grieving

friends and a familiar environment, we are stepping away from our childlike *self* and embracing the adult we're becoming. We all know the expectations of an adult includes finding work that supports you financially, moving out of your family home, and paving the way to become a responsible, contributing member of society. Yet it is possible that a person doesn't feel properly prepared to accept the requirements of this next stage and begins to search for someone else to maintain their accountability and responsibility. Yet another good reason to acknowledge the whole of changes in life.

Have you acknowledged the loss of a dream that could never be achieved? Was it a relationship that never reached that place of harmony and acceptance you so deserved? Did you have to agree to leave someone, an organization, or an environment, just to survive injury, trauma, or abuse? Did you feel cheated and tricked when you were certain that it was safe to be vulnerable? Has your pain been intruding on who you are as a person and preventing you from moving forward? Did you finally realize you may have been grieving for years and that much of what you carry with you each day is becoming more complex?

In the Bible, we learn that to everything there is a season and a time for every purpose. There is "A time to weep and a time to laugh; a time to mourn and a time to dance…"[35] This haunting passage implies that none of us are free from loss, but all of us have choices in how we live through it. However, grief over the loss is there just the same. We might tuck it away sometimes, ignoring our feelings as we move on, sometimes not even stopping long enough to acknowledge that we're no longer who we used to be, yet it's still there. Yes, loss easily changes us.

Was your loss the death of a significant person who filled your life with purpose and meaning? Was it a pet who loved you unconditionally through difficult times? Is it possible the pain was too great to know where to begin and the longer you waited to express it, the more frightening it became? Perhaps your tendency was to push through or ignore your feelings and merely attempt to turn the page, only this time the feelings you've amassed can't be ignored?

In being present to many dying people and their survivors, I would often hear family and friends' attempts to define or place value on a particular loss. From this I learned to live by the saying, "The greatest loss is the death of thee and me." To me, this phrase represents the fact that all loss has meaning and value and cannot be measured. Is it *your* death that you grieve, one that you realize has now become a reality, a period at the end of a sentence, a time that people acknowledge will happen in the not-too-distant future?

The Feelings Associated with Grief and Loss

The feelings of grief and loss are provocative. Loss is one of those life experiences that we imagine will happen to someone else and not ourselves. In the normal scheme of things, young people—who often deem themselves invincible—will often expect to reach adulthood and probably marry, succeed in their work, and bear children. At some time later in life, they will enjoy the marriage of their children, welcome grandchildren, and then experience joys of retirement. As we look forward to these stages of life, rarely do we contemplate death. However, it takes only one event, one loss, to shake a person, a family, and a community back to reality.

In fact, there is a phrase known in the field of psychology, the "crisis of the knowledge of death," which occurs when individuals are presented with situations where they are forced to accept the reality of loss. A tragic car accident, a natural disaster like a tornado or earthquake, or a terrorist attack can cause a dramatic shattering of an existential denial system that had been preserving a person's belief that no harm can come to them. The death of our parents represents the loss of history, part of our past and traditions. Yet most spend a lifetime preparing for this inevitable occurrence. The loss of a spouse or sibling represents the loss of our present and likely one that will alter many parts of the life we live each day. While some cannot even bear the thought of a parent or sibling dying, the death of our young causes a break in the order of life and death.

I have seen it again and again where families and colleagues gather, hoping to insulate their children and family members from the pain of their grief. When a child dies in a community, you can almost hear the silent prayer of gratitude when another parent realizes it was not their child. We know there is a natural order of things and as a result find it especially disturbing when young couples suddenly lose a spouse or parents outlive their children.

The death of a child is likely one of the most traumatic of all death experiences. While it's never been written in stone, we all enter a trust that children are simply not supposed to die before their parents. Whether the death is from the inability to conceive a much-wanted baby, a miscarriage, known as a spontaneous abortion, a planned abortion, or the death of a child at any age, it is said that this represents the loss of future dreams and experiences. When a child is gone, families have only the past and may never be able to fully resolve the emptiness and longing they are left with. There is a desire to keep the child's memory alive by talking about who they were and what they represented to the family while at the same time, the sorrow, anger, and despair unravels the ability to communicate thoughts and feelings.

Common to any loss, but in particular the sudden loss of a child, is the question, "How could this happen?" Families ask, "Why us, why our child, and why now?"

Chapter 7: On Grieving

Anger easily develops and couples find difficulty in reaching peace, at times, even from any support they may offer each other. As a result, another complex problem may emerge when either parent questions the effort being offered. Because individuals grieve in their own time and their own way, resentment may occur if one parent or family member feels the need to return to the life they had before the loss.

The common stereotype is the man in the family returning to work rather than staying at home to grieve with others. This hardly means that the person is done grieving but may in fact represent their best effort to cope with a situation that is inconceivable and unmanageable. Unfortunately, this action may be interpreted as abandonment and perceived as another loss from those around them. Therefore, it can often happen that, during times of grief, parents find it difficult to remain in their marital relationship. Blame for the loss or unresolved issues from the marriage may contribute to the need to flee.

Yet for some, if they can resolve their issues of guilt or tendency to hold the other responsible, their bond becomes stronger. These couples recognize that there is no other person in the world who understands the pain they have experienced. They rely on a unified hope that together they will someday be able to cope.

Whether acknowledged or spoken, people experience a variety of emotions in light of a loss. They often vacillate between anger, blame, sadness, and disappointment that the loss or death has occurred. While clearly not reality-based, they feel impotent and defeated in that they could not stop this experience from happening. At times they may even seem irrational.

A most prominent emotional occurrence following loss is a feeling of numbness, a sense of entering an emotionless, anesthetized, blunted state of being. Many people who are grieving describe an absence of color in their world and impart an experience of living under a veil where they see things from a different perspective. On several occasions I heard this comment from widows experiencing the loss of a beloved husband. It was often months and years later that they realized they were simply walking through their life but failing to notice they could not see beyond this 'veil.' They guessed it was there to protect them from any additional pain.

The lack of emotion is in and of itself disorienting and frightening, which can lead the person to develop a lack of trust in their own judgement. Grief-stricken people describe a change in their mental ability, for instance, difficulty with simple math exercises like balancing a checkbook or determining the percentage of a tip.

The grieving person may also find themselves being insensitive or unfeeling to others around them. This can be awkward because people tend to reach out to others in grief to provide support. Our culture has not been successful in finding ways to deal with loss. As a result, feeling unprepared and inadequate to find the words to help, visitors end up telling their own grief story. While their intent is to offer their understanding through their own experience, the grieving person generally has little energy to support another and may seem uncaring or unappreciative of the encounter. Therefore, the best one can do when a person is grieving a loss is to be present and accepting. The last thing that is helpful is to describe your own loss.

Death presents so many uncertainties that friends and community members often struggle with the appropriate response in offering any assistance. Frequently they attempt to support others by offering food as a gesture of their caring. Americans are known to prepare casserole dishes or meals for families or persons going through hard times. Providing a grieving family food means that's one less part of daily life they have to think about. While a wife and mother may deny herself of food, it may suddenly become clear that the children in the family have a need to eat.

In one instance with a family from a non-American background, the thought of taking food during the time of mourning stimulated tremendous anger from the wife. She became anxious and tearful yelling out to everyone who would listen, "My husband will never have a cheeseburger again. And neither will I!" This represented the awareness and possibility of irrational thoughts when facing the pain of grief. It required considerable coaching for this woman to be free of the need to deprive herself because her husband had died.

People who are grieving sometimes are motivated to seek help after recognizing the countless changes they see in themselves along with the many questions they have about the possibility of ever being happy again. This is a time when they may be open to support. When there is evidence of a strong faith tradition throughout life, a person in mourning will commonly want to rely on their belief system to support themselves through a loss.

As a member of a trauma support team, I did everything in my power to assess whether the family was known by a local faith community. Especially with trauma, the teams were often aware and able to predict when a patient's condition would end in death. This provided an opportunity to align with the support of the rabbi, priest, or minister who could be there at the hospital before the patient died.

In one case, a young man had been in a terrible vehicle accident when his car hit a tree. This incident essentially left him with minimal and diminishing brain function. The challenge to communicate this information to the family was intensified by the fact that each family member spoke only Portuguese. Fortunately, a young Portuguese priest from their church responded to our call and arrived immediately to make the necessary connections with the family. Standing by the priest's side, the doctor and I were able to relay the seriousness of the situation.

Chapter 7: On Grieving

Knowing I worked in the area of death and dying, the chief of trauma service always accepted my cues to take the necessary time to allow families to realize what they were facing. The physicians would proceed with their formal brain death protocol, testing to determine any chance for sustained life. In the meantime, the priest and I supported each step with the family until we all returned to deliver the bad news. By this time the family knew each care provider and we knew them. It made it meaningful as they could see that we understood their pain.

It was the late Rev. William Sloane Coffin, former senior minister at the Riverside Church in New York City who became a model to many of us through his eulogy to his beloved son, Alex. Alex died in a car accident in 1983 when he was 24 years old. Coffin described him as "fair as a star when only one is shining in the sky."

Because of Coffin's position, many questioned how God allowed this to happen to him. Coffin had devoted himself to the church and many humanitarian causes including the CIA and his direct support to General Patton. At considerable risk to his own personal safety, he joined the Freedom Riders in the South, mixed-race groups who deliberately defied the region's segregation laws. He held a long history where his beliefs took on a life of their own. His courageous nature was evident in his engagement in resistance movements, the Peace Corps, and working for the release of Americans being held unjustly throughout the world.

This time, his son's death was out of his control. Yet in response to people who wanted to blame God for this tragedy, Coffin reminded us that:

> "My own consolation lies in knowing that it was not the will of God that Alex die; that when the waves closed over the sinking car, God's heart was the first of all our hearts to break."

Because loss and the experience of death is so prominent in my work, it is difficult for me to speak solely about loss without reminding you about the joy of love. Loving someone creates a space where, forever and a day, you are vulnerable to the possibility of loss and the pain of grief. No one can predict if a relationship will last forever or, as Coffin also said, "a person may race you to the grave."

But death is only one aspect of loss in a relationship. We have a choice to remain accountable and responsible to both our needs and the needs of others. Being challenged by our spirit to be the best we can be opens our world to the possibility that, at times, we may fail or even disappoint ourselves or another individual. Much can be learned by being committed to a life of honesty and openness. It can be frightening or even painful to acknowledge when there is dissonance in a relationship. But communication is a great healer. When couples, families, and friends become used to hearing our thoughts and opinions with the intention to grow and support the relationship, it becomes a norm to be used by everyone in our world.

The Awareness of Grief

Since grief seems to be something we might carry around and often avoid addressing, it is significant to assess the areas of our life and history that hold tension from unresolved or anticipatory loss or grief. This lesson is an important one. The experience of loss, death, and dying clearly has a potential to create change in each of us.

While we can't escape the potential for loss, each of us has a choice in how we proceed through the experience of living. Accepting the reality of death may alter our relationship with the present; this awareness recognizes and provides an appreciation in the limitation of our time in life with people who matter and whom we love. When we fail to admit that there is a beginning and an end, life and the relationships we value are too often taken for granted. There actually could be some benefit to remaining conscious and aware of this most painful of life's experiences. It is well-known that when we disown parts of ourselves, we risk the potential for acting out the feelings associated with these parts. In a similar manner, an acceptance or facing our fears about loss may free us to live our lives with greater appreciation and passion.

When you recognize that life is not a forever thing and more precious than you ever imagined, you may use this awareness to take greater responsibility in addressing thoughts and feelings in a more timely fashion. For example, since most of us don't express our anger well, we often send people away in order to avoid confrontation and are unwilling to resolve the anger and hurt. Next time this happens to you, imagine that if death suddenly and unexpectedly occurred, how would you prefer your last words and last emotions shared with that person to be?

At work, we may find unresolved or anticipatory grief taking hold and contributing to much of the acting out and positioning I've spoken about. Concerns mounting from the anticipatory fear of losing a position or no longer being that "top dog" admired by administrators can unleash a set of disarming behaviors. I've said this before: People strive to do the best they can do in life; that means being the best child, the best parent, the best spouse, or the best employee. There are times in life when we put unnecessary stress on ourselves and others and simply forget to live with the understanding that life has gains and sometimes losses, doing anything in our power to "win."

When grief is left unattended, it has a tendency to intrude upon you and your ability to accept things in life. If we come from a posture of fear, we may have feelings that resemble the feelings of loss. That void or pit in your stomach may rise and frighten you and disarm you. Just as it can be difficult to distinguish between excitement and fear, the feelings of unresolved grief can leave a person worried that harm is about to emerge. Don't let old grief and loss prevent you from living your life by taking risks around love and taking action.

The next part of this chapter will allow you to do an audit of sorts. If we agree that many of us fail to address our losses and that we easily bring forth the pain of loss, this exercise will allow you to place your thoughts and feelings down on paper and address each experience, so that you can let it set you free.

Actual Experiences with Any Death or Loss:

Name the person or event and provide an approximate date of the loss. Provide some details describing your relationship to the person or lost object. Acknowledge any evidence of leftover feelings or regrets. Create a separate document if you need more space to write.

1. _____
_____
_____
_____
_____

2. _____
_____
_____
_____
_____

3. _____
_____
_____
_____
_____

4. _____
_____
_____
_____
_____

5._____

Anticipated Experiences with Death or Loss:

Anticipatory grief occurs any time there is a *threat* of loss. The experience occurs before death and can easily happen when a loved one is in any phase of a chronic progressive illness such as Parkinson's or Alzheimer's disease or in the case of a diagnosis that has a defined end to life. Symptoms rob the individual of their role relationship due to limitations in mobility or communication or pain. While anticipatory grieving can assist individuals in acceptance and reaching closure, it does not replace grieving after death. Consider whether you have any concerns over anticipatory loss.

1._____

2._____

3._____

Chapter 7: On Grieving

4. _____
_____
_____
_____
_____

5. _____
_____
_____
_____
_____

Episodes of Unresolved Grief:

Please explain what may have contributed to this. Here are some examples:

I have difficulty speaking about the person who has died.
I have difficulty falling asleep, staying asleep, or find myself sleeping at times I need to be awake.
I find people don't know what to say to me about my loss.
I prefer to be alone.
I am losing/gaining weight.
I have difficulty concentrating and solving simple problems.
I seem to have lost my interest in things.
I don't really care if something happens to me.
My body feels heavy.
I have been unable to cry.
I cry all the time without much control.
I have a lump in my throat when I think about my loss.
I don't know when I should discard clothing and personal belongings.
I am anxious all the time.
I try to support others in their grieving and not show my pain.

1. _____
_____
_____
_____
_____

2. _____
_____
_____
_____
_____

3. _____
_____
_____
_____
_____

4. _____
_____
_____
_____
_____

Transitions That Create an Experience of Loss:

While not a death, transitions that occur throughout our life, and the life of family before us, often escape our awareness as being a significant loss. We are a society characterized by supportive, loving parents, or sometimes hovering parents who may overprotect their children to avoid pain or suffer disappointment. The result? An entire generation who steps away from challenges when pain and discomfort arise. In turn, these occurrences can silently and sometimes unconsciously impact some of your decisions about how to proceed in life.

Consider all the situations that may have been unsettling. Was there prolonged sickness in your household? Was there a death or a divorce while you were growing up? Did anything impact your ability to launch to another stage of life? Did family have difficulty addressing grief?

Examples of transitions that can impact grief:

Moving to a new state/home
Changing schools
Loss of a job

Chapter 7: On Grieving

Graduation
Marriage
Change in financial security
Divorce
Loss of limb/body part
Loss of an important object
Threats to safety: 9/11, war, school shootings, COVID-19

In reviewing all the possibilities that times of transition may have challenged you, begin to journal any and all transitions occurring in your life. Provide as much detail as you can remember. Honor any feelings of loss that may emerge as you tap into these memories. Name your feelings and whether you received support to grieve.

_____
_____
_____
_____
_____
_____
_____
_____
_____
_____
_____
_____
_____
_____
_____
_____
_____
_____
_____
_____
_____
_____
_____
_____
_____
_____
_____

The Ultimate Loss: The Death of Me

In maintaining my own healing practice and in the process of writing this book, I kept one important premise in mind: Provide a loving environment and people will respond. I firmly believe that each of you are here for a purpose and that embracing this belief will help you understand that the world is a far better place because you are here. Whether in my therapy practice where the agenda was generally grief and loss or in corporate life where the primary intent was to serve as an expert in the standardization and documentation of patient care, I insisted on being the same person. I remained open and accepting, sharing information, looking for opportunities to help people grow through support and praise and to comfort and encourage others to find themselves despite their pain and loss.

I lived by the words of many much wiser than myself, but here I share with you the wisdom of the Dutch Catholic priest, professor, writer, and theologian Henri Nouwen, who asked:

> *"Did I offer peace today? Did I bring a smile to someone's face? Did I say words of healing? Did I let go of my anger and resentment? Did I forgive? Did I love? These are the real questions. I must trust that the little bit of love that I sow now will bear many fruits, here in this world and the life to come."*

I feel grateful that although I had a difficult beginning with the illness and death of my father during my teen years, I became more alert to recognize the pain in others. I found myself seeking isolation so that I would not cause any additional burden to my family. I worked diligently in school to make them proud, although everyone was too busy to notice.

I am proof that out of early struggles, a person can not only turn life around, but use these experiences to become an instrument of love and change. I learned to watch for signs of grief in others and remain vigilant to this day. As a result, this book emerged out of a request from many colleagues and clients to leave a legacy, and it is my gift to all who choose to read it. It is proof that you can learn more about yourself and even uncover hidden parts of yourself so that your relationships will become even richer. The ability to be honest with yourself and others allows you to develop relationships that are meaningful and loving. Yes, I encourage you to look within and define who you want to be. Once this is done you have greater control over choosing to have the right people in your life at the right time.

As I have professed through life, it is important to feel your feelings of grief, love, and sadness, as well as anger, making every effort to address anything that may create distance between you and people important to you. Acknowledging loss and accepting the pain allows you to consider a life, albeit different, when someone you love is gone. That is when you discover who you are.

Chapter 7: On Grieving

This time, the death I'm experiencing is the death of me.

I am told that having stage 3c ovarian cancer places me in a statistical body of knowledge that more clearly defines when my life will end. In stage 3 ovarian cancer, the cancer is found in one or both ovaries, as well as in the lining of the abdomen, or it has spread to lymph nodes in the abdomen. Stage 3c means that larger deposits of cancer cells are found outside the spleen or liver, or that it has spread to the lymph nodes.

For me it all started with a belief that I had an abdominal hernia, a rather benign concern that I was assured could wait a year while I completed an important project in another state. The hernia operation became a TV drama when the doctor entered the post anesthesia care unit telling me he had to "open and close me" as I required another more extensive surgery. He had already begun to arrange the assistance of a second physician who specialized in gynecological oncology. Apparently, my ovaries were wrapped in the lining of the abdomen, the omentum, and presented high up around my stomach.

I now know full well the pain of the anticipatory loss of me. I was informed that even with surgery and chemotherapy, the life expectancy is four years. While I am fighting this cancer and agreeing to all the necessary surgeries and chemotherapy infusions, there is greater awareness of the uncertainty of survival. I want to prove the statistics wrong and so, all the while, when I could raise my head out of the stupor imposed by chemotherapy agents needed to kill cancer cells, I have been writing vigorously to fill my days with purpose.

For someone who has sat at the bedside of so many as they approached their death and supported others at the death of someone they loved, expecting death to be close by is quite a different experience for me. I am satisfied that I have led a life of more fulfillment than I ever imagined. I have truly been loved and continue to be loved and accepted despite my current condition. I lived through the arduous effort to become a professional and to engage in opportunities to learn and to teach. I always insisted on the best quality care that could be offered to my patients. I was always the one who would find her voice and speak up for those who could not speak. Now the tides have turned, and I am the receiver of healthcare. I am the one who gets in the bed, gets hooked up to IVs every three weeks with the hope to combat this disease. But even still, I am, as always, going to be the one to help others prepare for their death as they observe the passing of my time.

As I proceed through this journey, I am aware of the sadness—quickly followed by incredible frustration—that prevents me from controlling so many things. Chemotherapy has left me with a significant case of neuropathy in my hands, feet, and legs. I never knew what that meant until becoming aware of a total lack of sensation. It has compromised my balance, making it difficult to walk the length of my home and definitely the great outdoors. So walking is a challenge. This angers me, makes me anxious, and sometimes frightens me if I let it. So, I need not let it. I cannot control the fact that I have cancer and that I am likely going to die sooner than I expected, but I can control how I live.

I try my very best to take time to grieve and feel my feelings. The awareness that each time I look into the face of someone I love may be one of the last makes this especially important. So, how do I cope with this? I have taken responsibility to say all that I can think to say to each person directly. I try to convey the meaning they hold for me and the wishes I have for them. George and I plan visits. I understand how easy it is to deny anticipatory loss, so we are not waiting until it is convenient for someone to come to us.

While I am told I look good now that my hair has returned, this outward sign makes it easy for others to believe this is all going to go away. However, not for me. I am well aware that time is precious, and so we are making visits to loved ones to enable me to say goodbye. In some cases, it's hello and goodbye for some relatives we haven't seen in so long.

The times of deep sadness are generally saved for the middle of the night. I have depression—I like to say, depression with a little "d," not a big "D," i.e., not an official diagnosis. My depression is an aspect of my grief and I view it as normal. The time of most difficulty is thinking about all the stages of life I will miss in my future. It is likely I won't see my grandchildren graduate or get married or have children of their own. I won't be there for my children as they age or support my dear husband as he gets closer to his time of dying.

These thoughts bring me to tears and place a lump in my throat that I've never experienced before. These are the loves of my life, and not being here with them gives me the most pain. When I cannot deal with the amount of pain I feel, I do know that I can change my thoughts, stay in the present, and be grateful for what is before me today.

No, I am not dying today and there is another chance to hug my husband and hold my kids tightly. I will do this as long as life allows.

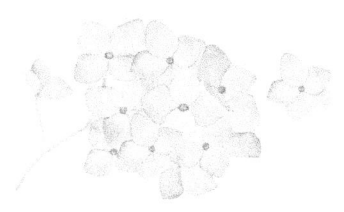

The Path of Resilience

In his book, *Man's Search for Meaning*, Viktor Frankl, a survivor of imprisonment in four different concentration camps, termed the experience of "existential frustration" as the moment at which an individual questions their very foundation and whether this life has any meaning, purpose, or value.[36] Frankl goes into great detail about the human responses he experienced in himself and others when trying to overcome difficult situations as well as combat the range of emotions—from apathy to the ultimate of all losses, "emotional death."

Emotional death occurs when all feeling is blunted in order to face the merciless and brutal treatment occurring before an individual. It seems that one of the most prominent techniques used by the Nazis overseeing concentration camps was an attempt to dehumanize their prisoners, to not only strip them of their clothes and possessions, but anything and anyone that defined them. Being in a situation that is totally beyond your control can take away everything that you possess—that is, except your ability to choose how you deal with it.

More times than I can count, people have come into my life at times of great despair. They may have a loss or struggle with a decision that presents uneasiness and fear. Some define a conflict that takes them out of their safe place and challenges their integrity and security. I've listened to the experiences of war and the guilt that placed our soldiers in a state of traumatic stress and disrepair in mind, body, and spirit. I've heard them describe their self-imposed prison in their basements as they feared their own behavior during flashbacks when they recalled the killing of children that could have been their own. I've listened to mothers and shared their tears as they described the need to terminate their much-wanted pregnancy after learning they were carrying an anencephalic child, a fatal condition in which a baby is born with an underdeveloped brain and an incomplete skull. I've learned firsthand the courage it takes to let your loved ones go and allow them to be removed from life support when the choice of life is no longer possible.

When working with clients and through my own experiences, I learned never to judge others' decisions and choices in the presence of loss. The pain of loss is quite real. It changes a person and makes them vulnerable. Out of this awareness are many opportunities to offer forgiveness. First, we need to forgive ourselves for not always being as sharp and capable as we might like. Then we need to learn to forgive others, especially when they fail to meet our expectations when we have been silently keeping our pain to ourselves.

I have yet to meet a person who has lived a life of utter peace and tranquility, an existence without one blemish. From the outside, people may appear to have the right physique, the best clothes, money to spare, the job that suits them, and a loving family—the "perfect package" so to speak. Have they truly managed to skirt all controversy and loss? Of course not. But is it possible that they have redefined what truly matters and found ways for acceptance? This can give us all hope.

Psychologists tell us that resilient individuals are known to use skills to reframe their condition and find meaning that energizes them, allowing a return to a sense of hope, well-being, and survival. This learned process allows us to change our feelings by controlling our thinking. For example, if overcome by anger or sadness, it is possible to get relief by merely changing our thoughts. This is the exact mechanism I find most useful when I, too, am overwhelmed by losses during my cancer treatment.

Some call this I/E or "intellect over emotion." In the highly intellectualized culture in which we live, many people do not know what to do with the emotion of anger. In fact, our culture has difficulty with many powerful emotions. In toddlerhood, expressing anger or sadness may have bought a seat in the corner until our parent or caregiver perceived we could regain control. So, it's no surprise that many people have limited practice in expressing their anger as well as finding it capable of being a positive recourse. Yet, anger and sadness are major manifestations of grief. In order to reach a place of resilience, it is necessary to find a means to express our emotions in a positive, creative, and healing fashion.

The Instinct to Cope

By now you are understanding that life offers many opportunities to heal and that grief, which is a part of loss, is unlike clinical depression. Among several findings in the *Diagnostic and Statistical Manual of Mental Disorders*, depression demonstrates a "markedly diminished interest or pleasure in all, or almost all, activities most of the day, nearly every day."[37] This is very different from grief, which allows you to experience both joy and sadness. In fact, common to the grieving process are the times when individuals and families call upon memories that allow them to laugh and cry. This is particularly the case in certain cultures that celebrate a person's life as early as the day of the wake. In fact, my husband's family who descended from Scotland were known to spend more time at the corner bar than in the midst of grievers in a funeral home. Raising a glass with each other became an important ritual allowing men in the family to find an acceptable way to release their experience of grief.

Tradition becomes an important element in the effort to cope as well. The Italians of my forefathers and mothers had many distinct traditions including hiring people to wail at the funeral. These were people hired by the family to provide additional mourners to show respect to the dead person and to help others engage in feelings of deep sadness as the wailers did their job. Today, Italians do what they do best and that is to join together with family at the dinner table.

Despite this awareness, through a natural resistance to avoid pain of any kind, human beings have the tendency to elude the feelings of grief and loss. You might agree to attend a service or even support the writing of a eulogy, yet that doesn't mean you're done grieving; grieving is not a one-time thing. Previously it was men that denied their grief by simply turning a page in their history without feeling their feelings. However, women do this too as they observe a similar style of coping when they need to return to work or their daily routine. When it comes to avoidance, the reasons are countless; living in sadness leaves people feeling unproductive and vulnerable, and who wants to feel that way?

You, too, may be carrying grief, not only from your personal past but also from your family's collective past. I am convinced that we grieve the events faced by family members as vividly as events that impact us personally. What did it feel like to learn that your grandparents struggled as they crossed the Atlantic in the steerage of a ship, some only to be turned away because the family member serving as their sponsor never received the letter to be at the pier to welcome them? Or that your ancestors endured concentration camps?

My dear friend tells the story of her mother and aunt who, as children, were sent away on one of the last *kindertransports*. They traveled alone by train in order to be saved from an unspeakable death, never knowing if they would see their parents again. I've often wondered, how has this personal grief story affected my friend's life? This experience had to have multiple recognizable and not so imperceptible responses through the lives of this and many families.

You might ask, why do we avoid our time of grieving? It is understandable. The depths of loss can be so great that the pain can be unbearable. I have heard friends and family admit that they "simply don't have time." In fact, what they mean to say is that they are afraid to go to that place of vulnerability; once they open their mind and body, they fear the feelings will flood over them, get out of control, and become unstoppable.

Whether it's a deep and frightening experience of loneliness and uncertainty or the many other challenges that occur during anyone's lifetime, life presents us with events that are unimaginable and for which we may feel unprepared. Some are completely unexpected while others may occur over time. It doesn't matter. When an incident occurs to the extent that it requires some distinct energy to resolve or just survive, you—in all of your humanity—face a choice of allowing the aftermath to overcome you or finding a way to bounce back.

Out of all loss comes potential and choice based on what life lessons you have learned. Life is full of choices and an equal number of unknowns. You would think that before reaching out on new adventures or taking a new path, you would be certain that the road is safe, a road recently paved—all the potholes covered with a sufficient layer of new asphalt. However, all the preparation and consideration of every possibility cannot truly prepare us for the unknowns. Just as we may see a caution sign warning us about flooding, there is no guarantee that individuals will heed the warning. While we may be able to consider the possibilities or prepare for crises, we still won't be 100 percent sure we have what it takes to get through a difficult time.

Ignoring warning signs may create situations where you find yourself swept away in currents over which you have no control. Yet, it is amazing that despite these warnings, humans continue to insist they can defy reason. As a therapist, I experienced people in shock and dismay that a particular situation actually happened to them. Yet in truth, with all the potential to learn to be vigilant, other parts of them took over and denial set in. Ego sometimes gets in the way of believing that the same rules apply to many people. For instance if a person is unfaithful, it will only last so long before their partner notices warning signs and starts to question the indiscretion.

What you *do* have is the work at hand. You are now practicing a new way of being where you openly question your part in every situation you must face. You instinctively ask the questions about your responsibility and accountability. You may now appreciate that other people have an equal responsibility to accept their part. You are better able to define what motivates you by having a better understanding of your needs, your abilities, your opinions, your beliefs, and your limitations. And in addition, there is an awareness that, at times, you may be blinded to a part of yourself and need to trust others who may see you better than you see yourself.

Openness often means taking an active role in coming out of isolation. It requires risk to be willing to consider the thoughts and feelings of others. When alone, there is a tendency to be void of feedback. If you are angry and negative, you tend to remain in this mindset and build a belief system that supports your anger and mistrust of others.

Resilience in the Workplace

Working as a manager for a national consulting company, my director, Liz, and I recognized symptoms of apathy and loss within a consultant working on one of our hospital assignments. The consultant, whom we will call John to maintain anonymity, had been working with a client as their clinical informaticist. His job was to support the transformation of a standardized documentation system which would also be converted to an electronic format. This effort required diligence, commitment, and an ability to work in environments often intolerant to change. John needed to interface with hospital leaders at the local level and the national office. This multi-billion-dollar project was part of a 70-hospital national healthcare system demonstrating uniformity in care as a process improvement.

Liz had been warned by the client that John was not meeting the expected standards of performance and that his job was in jeopardy. While I had never had the opportunity to set eyes on this individual, we heard enough that made it clear to us both that something dramatic needed to occur to turn this situation around. The hospital CEO was complaining to the national office of the project on a daily basis. This only accelerated stress to the degree that John was finding it even more difficult to function.

This was one of those times when a miracle was needed. I can remember thinking of the phrase, "When the going gets tough the tough get going."[38] The proverb was attributed to Joseph P. Kennedy, the father of President John F. Kennedy, and intimated that in spite of critical times and situations, people who are strong-willed and tough see opportunities that others miss. Liz and I made our way by plane and car to meet with John during his lunch break. He suspected this visit would end in his termination.

After listening carefully and hearing his level of honesty and humility, we determined that he had so many untapped qualities that it was worth starting from scratch and building him up to a place where he could appreciate himself again. Instinctively we knew that if John could see this, his performance would improve.

> "When the going gets tough the tough get going."
> —*Joseph P. Kennedy*

Together, we developed and remained true to a plan that included daily interventions and the completion of a program I had developed to support training for consultants called *Consulting Excellence*. The plan worked only because John embraced the effort he needed to take with full mind and spirit.

Many years later, while I continue to praise him, he insists on recognizing my willingness to believe in his ability along with the enthusiasm to help him turn his life around. He insisted I tell his story and share the following email:

> "…I had a unique experience with love in the form of compassion and empathy that was shown toward me in a professional setting. The love I speak about is so powerful and dynamic that it can overwhelm the recipient of such emotion and power. Love doesn't see race, natural origin, sexual orientation, or any of the other dynamics in life that we decide to allow to be barriers to us getting to know one another. I met a woman who had so much love with no judgement and no preconditions that at first, I didn't think the love was real. I was in a situation where I didn't understand the job that was required of me. A lady named Ellen came in as a new supervisor on my job. She was very kind and very personable, but at the end of the day she had a job to do.
>
> …Instead of following the directive to terminate me, Ellen decided to assist me in changing my course of direction and showing me how to perform at a level that was acceptable for the position that I was being paid for. Ellen did not know me and had no previous experience working with me. All she knew was that I was an employee of hers that needed assistance and she reached out to help me versus following normal business trends when an employee underperforms.
>
> …She saved my career. She allowed me to move into very powerful positions at large organizations and I know I would not have been able to have the success that I've had without her.
>
> …Ellen Reed's attitude and conscientiousness is contagious to all individuals who interact with her. This level of passion toward humanity cannot be taught, nor can you pretend to possess this gift of empathy."
>
> —*John (Anonymous)*

Chapter 8: The Path of Resilience

To this day, I remain humbled and honored to have been a part of John's success. John was so close to losing everything—including the potential loss of security at a stage in his life when he was raising a family. At times we act out of fear, rejection, or a long history of not being accepted. Regretfully, a consistent message can also prevent a person from experiencing the need to belong. With his feeling of "not being good enough"—which can take place for generations—my job was to help John rid himself of this fatalistic way of thinking and acting and acknowledge who he truly was so that he could do his job. I became a vessel to remind him that, despite all that had occurred, he was loved and appreciated. He needed to recognize the shame, fear, guilt, and sadness (which may not have even been his) and after acknowledging its origin, separate from it.

There is no doubt in my mind that his faith, his attitude, and renewed understanding of his worth allowed John to see things from a new perspective and demonstrate an ability and desire to succeed. Of course, I believe it was always present within him.

In essence, this is an example of resilience. It is a process of adapting well in the face of adversity, trauma, tragedy, loss, or anticipated loss. It can arise out of any threat—to a family, relationships within the family, a workplace situation, financial insecurity (either real or projected), or most especially, from serious health issues. The most encouraging thing about resilience is it is a trait that can be achieved by anyone and is hardly unique to a small subset of any culture. Much like grief, resilience has components in thoughts, feelings, and actions, and is a characteristic that can be learned and developed by any one of us. As a result, resilience gives much hope during times of loss or crisis; it can allow individuals, families, and groups to make major changes in their lives to support and enable a positive outcome.

The Path of Resilience

Perhaps you have never explored this part of yourself and imagined you might address resilience only after being faced with a hardship or difficult life situation. Actually, a more contemporary belief supports the benefit of developing skills in resilience at any time in our lives. Some of the newest and most exciting scientific findings about the brain indicate that the human brain can change and learn new patterns of response to traumatic life events. This is conceptualized through discoveries related to a scientific concept called neuroplasticity.

With research dating back as far as the 1700s, it wasn't until the advent of combined efforts in biological, psychological, medical, and spiritual research that scientists began to appreciate the possibilities being considered for future discovery in brain function that has had major impact toward understanding Alzheimer's disease, autism, brain trauma, aging, and the many faces of resilience.

In an online video course provided by the World Science Festival, Dr. Fran Norris, a social psychologist and professor studying human resilience at Dartmouth's Medical School of Psychiatry, indicated without hesitation that resilience is a *process*, not an outcome.[39] This finding reinforces the idea that human beings can develop the ability to store the necessary brain function to overcome the phenomena of tremendous loss. It also supports that it can be done at any time, including during early development when the brain is still in flux.

Thus, "bouncing back" indicates that there are many reasons a person needs to develop their resilience capacity. This can be done through their ability to actively address this important concept, to gain a storehouse of knowledge about it, and to change their belief and mindset to understand that, through life, it *is* possible to reconstitute and even experience a better perception of life after a tremendous, life-changing event.

I believe that young children can be provided with examples of loss and begin to address more benign or less traumatic experiences that can prepare them for struggles down the road. Intuitively, as a grief therapist, I would do my best to prepare my own children for the inevitable experience of loss. Having had this denied to me as a child, it reinforced my belief that my children have the tools to address their pain.

In a simple, unsuspecting manner, the boys and I would address the death of animals in the road. In that they had no particular personal connection to these beings, it served as a non-threatening way to introduce death and the faith we have when someone or something dies or is lost. For us this was heaven. As a mother, I would say a prayer for the dead animal's well-being and assure the boys that the squirrel's time or purpose in this life must have come to an end. When they were older and more capable to address the meaning of loss, I invited more discussion about what they experienced when loss occurred to them or those around them. This was the case when we moved from a town and a neighborhood filled with friends they loved and later with the death of their grandparents.

Consider that every disappointment—including and especially our collective experiences with loss—prepares and enables us to believe that we can survive beyond the deep internal pain we may feel. On 9/11, as two planes destroyed the World Trade Center Towers, the terrorists were certain that taking down the Towers would take down our nation. To the contrary for some, albeit a short-lived time, Americans joined together and remembered to support each other. Many of us returned home that night to be together with our children and spouses and attempted to reach out to anyone that mattered. Once again, we were given an opportunity to learn that no matter the issue stirring among us, never should we take for granted the people that make up this nation, our community, and our family.

Becoming a Resilient Human Being

While convincing ourselves that—from a physical and physiological perspective—our brain and the whole of our being are actively and instinctively trying to restore themselves in the face of tragedy, this is clearly not enough. As an individual you may want to consider taking a more active role in preparing for life events that require these necessary skills.

We build on our behavioral skills related to resilience each time we meet a new person, start a new job, travel to a new place, or experience any number of events. This includes openly verbalizing thoughts and feelings about situations before us that enable us to learn the perspective of others. Some of us are content to maintain the same pattern of behavior each day while others actively seek out new skills and encounters they hope to accomplish in life. An important factor is to evaluate openness to change, of course, always starting with you.

How would you rate your willingness to embrace change? Accepting change as part of being alive is a significant way to build coping skills. If even the slightest change creates stress, it is likely that a major unsuspected, unplanned change may be enough to raise your stress levels and place you in a state of distress. In 1967, psychiatrists Holmes and Rahe developed a study to determine whether stress had an impact on physical and mental illness. They learned that based on an inventory of stressors present at a given time, a score could establish the likelihood that stress could contribute to illness.[40] For this reason, it serves us all to remain aware of the mounting areas of stress in our lives.

The Holmes and Rahe Social Readjustment Scale

To use this research effectively, select the stressors you currently experience from the list on the next page and total the value. According to the research, your score determines a best estimate of an individual's tendency to be overwhelmed with change. The researchers indicate that this score could contribute to stress mounting to the level of illness.

STRESSORS	VALUE
1. Death of spouse	100
2. Divorce	73
3. Separation	65
4. Incarceration	63
5. Death of close family member	63
6. Personal injury or illness	53
7. Marriage	50
8. Job loss	47
9. Marital reconciliation	45
10. Retirement	45
11. Alteration in health of family member	44
12. Pregnancy	40
13. Sex problems	39
14. Addition of family members	39
15. Changes in business culture	39
16. Alteration in finances	38
17. Death of close friend	37
18. Alteration in work	36
19. Controversy with spouse	35
20. A large mortgage or loan	31
21. Foreclosure of mortgage or loan	30
22. Change in responsibilities at work	29
23. Children leaving home	29
24. Trouble with in-laws	29

25.	Outstanding personal achievement	28
26.	Spouse begins or stops work	26
27.	Graduation from school/ college	26
28.	Alteration in living conditions	25
29.	Change of personal habits	24
30.	Trouble with boss	23
31.	Change in work hours or conditions	20
32.	Moving to a new residence	20
33.	Transfer to a new school/ college	20
34.	Increase or decrease in recreation	19
35.	Change in church or associated activities	19
36.	Change in social activities	18
37.	Taking out a loan or mortgage	17
38.	Alteration in sleep patterns	16
39.	Change in number of family get-togethers	15
40.	Change in eating habits	15
41.	Vacation	13
42.	Christmas	12
43.	Minor violations of the law	11

Score	Comment
11-150	You have a low to moderate chance of becoming ill
151-299	You have a moderate to high chance of becoming ill
300-600	You have a high chance of becoming ill

How would you rate your willingness to embrace change?

List any events where you participated in a change over the past year. What was your role in promoting the change? Describe the outcome. Was there anything to gain?

_____
_____
_____
_____
_____
_____
_____
_____
_____
_____
_____
_____
_____
_____

As a new nursing practitioner, I began working in a hospital system well-known throughout the nation as having standardized practices. I quickly identified that while models of care were in place that allowed long-term employees a sense of confidence and competence, they no longer met quality measures supporting best practices. Arriving out of a university-based educational program that promoted our role as change agents, I often heard use of a concerning phrase that was a red flag: "We've always done it this way." It became clear that change would not come easy despite the many good arguments that were presented. As a result, when change was mandated by governing bodies, it created major disorganization in staff who tried their best to keep things the same.

Hopefully you will agree that accepting change is a mindset, one that can be learned and readjusted as a necessity of survival in life. Individuals who resist change fail to recognize that in most circumstances, when we give up something—even some old way of thinking—we open ourselves up to new (and sometimes better) opportunities.

Significant to your growth as an individual is the effort to build your personal resources, including and especially, your knowledge base about anything and everything you may need to prepare you to face the world. Let this be the time of your life when you start making better choices about what you need and want so that you can begin to develop these necessary tangible skills, for example, taking a long hard look at the way in which you spend money. Becoming debt-free is a goal that allows you a greater experience in safety and security, all building blocks for becoming the best you can be. Being diligent, accountable, and responsible for learning everything you need to know is a significant part of developing your personal repertoire, all those parts and pieces of who you are as an individual that you can eventually rely upon to provide confidence and competence.

> Individuals who resist change fail to recognize that in most circumstances, when we give up something—even some old way of thinking—we open ourselves up to new opportunities.

In these times, there are no excuses when you are determined to expand your knowledge base and to encourage those around you to do the same. If that means returning to school for a degree or an advanced degree, do it one or two classes at a time. If none of this is possible because of a financial hardship, explore every possibility, every scholarship or grant that may in fact be available just waiting to be utilized. If you have difficulty imagining finding the time, complete a time in motion inventory where you take account of all of your free time so that you can visualize exactly how you spend your time. This may allow you to become a better steward of your time in general, or it could spark conversations where you can ask for help to fulfill your dreams.

When all this fails, become an expert researcher of the internet. You live in a time when the world is truly open to you. As in the proverb, "The world is your oyster,"[41] you, too, can be that silent unsuspecting creature that's forming great beauty within.

A "Time in Motion Study" helps you consider your ability to maintain a healthy existence as you increase your awareness of potential stress. Many parts of your life are predetermined by responsibilities related to work and family. The following diagram may help you represent areas that require change to allow some room to live. Your new awareness may impact others' lives and serve as a place to begin to communicate your needs.

Time in Motion Study One Week

Time of day	Monday	Tuesday	Wednesday	Thursday	Friday	Saturday	Sunday
7am	Travel to work	Travel to work	Travel to work	Travel to work	Travel to work	Sleep	Sleep
8am	Work	Work	Work	Work	Work	Family Time	Family Time
9am	Work	Work	Work	Work	Work	Family Time	Family Time
10am	Work	Work	Work	Work	Work	Family Time	Family Time
11am	Work	Work	Work	Work	Work	Family Time	Family Time
12pm	Work	Work	Work	Work	Work	Lunch	Lunch
1pm	Work	Work	Work	Work	Work	School Work	School Work
2pm	Work	Work	Work	Work	Work	School Work	School Work
3pm	Work	Work	Work	Work	Work	School Work	School Work
4pm	Work	Work	Work	Work	Work	School Work	School Work
5pm	Pick up kids	Pick up kids	Pick up kids	Pick up kids	Pick up kids	School Work	School Work
6pm	Dinner	Dinner	Dinner	Dinner	Dinner	Dinner	Dinner
7pm	Help Kids with Homework	Help Kids with Homework	Help Kids with Homework	Help Kids with Homework	Help Kids with Homework	Family Time	Family Time
8pm	School	School	School	School	School	Family Time	Family Time
9pm	School	School	School	School	School	Family Time	Family Time
10pm	School	School	School	School	School	Family Time	Family Time
11pm	Sleep	Sleep	Sleep	Sleep	Sleep	Sleep	Sleep
12am	Sleep	Sleep	Sleep	Sleep	Sleep	Sleep	Sleep

Chapter 8: The Path of Resilience

Resilience can also require you to clean your personal home and relationships in your life. Review your Social Atom that you completed in Chapter 5 and determine if you have developed the goal of filling your life with loving people. Letting go of a relationship that has become more work than joy is an example. If you truly value a relationship, do the work you need to do to communicate clearly what you need in your current relationships. Be sure to ask significant others and friends if you are keeping up your part of the relationship. If you are searching for someone with whom you can share your life with, there may be an equal number of losses or attempts along the way until you find that special person you might one day call your *one and only*. The reality is a lesson you may have learned in kindergarten. You may not like everyone and everyone may not like you. However, in order to successfully engage in the possibility of a relationship, you have to take risks and sometimes come to terms with loss.

There are challenging times in every relationship, even those that are more permanent or long-lasting. We may feel misunderstood or alone in our thinking and need validation. Finding a way to turn both realistic and unrealistic expectations around will support our ability to cope.

In truth, not everyone is sensitive to our needs all of the time; we are not always clear about prioritizing and communicating when and how much we want others to support us. It requires resilience to accept the valleys in our relationships and be able to look beyond those times. Despite our best efforts to communicate our needs and wants, others may still disappoint. At times, being resilient may mean learning to pick your battles and be okay with loss.

When you address the components of loss, you will find a powerful underpinning in the experience of guilt, blame, anger, and sadness. These qualities are unavoidable in the reality of grief and loss and can occur out of everyday circumstances, especially when you perceive you are lacking control over some aspect of your life. Being resilient may require you to use your skills to put your thoughts and feelings into words. This in and of itself can sometimes create an environment of risk—there's a chance it can elevate the fear that others will not respond in corresponding ways.

In keeping with the desire to achieve resilience, you may need to become courageous and be the first to reach out to others, even in those moments when you experience fear rising up within you. Practicing this task makes it easier in the future when you begin to have better control and exercise tangible ways to support an improved ability to communicate.

Human beings have a unique ability to learn and demonstrate choice. The willingness to take in information and grow new and different perspectives around even the worst of situations present considerable possibilities and hope. The good news is that individuals lacking a genetic component to be resilient still have the opportunity to learn the behaviors and tasks necessary to live a life of resiliency.

The Accommodation and Preparation to Develop Resilience

- **Take inventory of your losses:** Use the tasks you completed in Chapter 7 that asked you to take an inventory of your losses. First and foremost, make an effort to account for all of the loss you have experienced in life. This includes the death of family members, friends, pets, and any traumatic events related to loss. Carefully review your effort to address these losses or your tendency to avoid the pain of grief. Consider your intellectualization of your feelings and your behavioral responses and any efforts to avoid your addressing the meaning of the loss. Look at conclusions or lessons that may have become part of you as a result of your lesson from grief. Take an active part in resolving your grief.

- **Acceptance:** Our instinctive efforts to cope include a tendency to deny anything that may hurt us. Some individuals may avoid all efforts to grieve by being absent to known traditions and processes that encourage individuals to address a response to actual or anticipatory loss. Staying away from the dying person or other grieving family members need not be interpreted as the person is uncaring or less intensely involved. However, it is important for each of us to approach loss with honesty. Death and loss of any kind is very painful when the person or circumstance holds meaning in your life. Going through this part of the process actually supports your resolution with the experience of grief. Participating in the dying process enables individuals to accept that at a particular time and place, life ceases to be. Traditions actually serve by acknowledging loss as a family and allow you to provide and receive much-needed support. Your absence at these events may also stimulate the additional pain of loss for those hoping to enter a place of shared grief with others who may be experiencing similar pain.

- **Resolution and forgiveness:** Resilient individuals learn to reach a conclusion to business left undone. In addition to our discussion related to loss, it is significant to resolve any outstanding occurrences where anger still looms in the relationship. It's difficult to find an adequate way to tell someone that something they have done angers you. You may couch it behind feelings of hurt and pain but anger itself comes in many forms—ranging from frustration to disappointment and rage. This can also occur when your behavior adds to someone's disappointment. Too often this phenomenon is left unsaid or incomplete. Years may go by in which individuals, family members, or groups hold onto feelings that cloud their experience of a person. You may be aware of this in your own life. Years may have passed, the disagreement may no longer matter, but the feelings of anger remain. This is housekeeping that needs to be done. Anger only hurts the person holding onto it and is an unnecessary burden that can prevent the return of joy with the person in question and in other areas of life.

- **Keep things in perspective:** Not every event in our life needs to be a crisis. Some things that happen to us are merely changes that occur as part of living. A perfect example is the change we experience during the aging process. A person may wake up each day and embrace their time as an opportunity to provide joy to their experience of life as well as sending out love and joy to others. It is always your choice and within your control to maintain a healthy, positive outlook despite any situation that may arise. Consider your happiness. What does it take to make you feel safe and secure? Are you clear about your finances or are you overextending? Are there options to address this? Have you considered the people and things that are really important to you and your welfare? You may need to take some risks and welcome some change into your life in order to achieve a greater sense of security. Remember Maslow's Hierarchy of Needs theory and consider ways to be the best you can be.

- **Set goals:** Setting concrete, actionable goals stimulates and encourages your skills and usefulness throughout your life. Plan an outing, call on your friends, remain physically active, and learn something new. If there is something you would like to change, consider the options and take baby steps. Most importantly, be that person that knows how to nurture a positive view of yourself.

- **Change your thoughts:** When you start to feel down, change your thoughts. You may not always be able to change your feelings in the moment, but you can change the thoughts that swirl around in your mind. You don't need to dwell on something that overpowers you and brings you down; you have control over your mindset. It's the way you choose to see events and respond to communication with others. If you're experiencing a bigger concern and the world gets you down, consider what is important *in this moment*? By taking that simple next step, you can gain back control and help shift your mindset. During the pandemic of 2020, many of us had to limit the amount of news broadcasts and media messages that we were consuming. In a similar vein, determine one thing that is important in your life and put your energy on making it the absolute best you can. Perhaps you can initiate a green project for your home, like finding a plant for your side table. If you are experiencing sadness, worry, or anticipatory grief, get up and consider an exercise that requires some focus or take a walk outside to let your mind wander. These activities may help you reconsider the same situation from a different perspective. It might also help to think back on past life lessons or prominent people in your life that you look up to, including the joy you may have received along the way. In doing so, you may find that some of your worries dissolve and change to thoughts of gratitude.

- **Love:** There are so many opportunities to give and receive love. Be on the lookout for these moments in your life and know that love may be in places you never considered before. Most of all, appreciate who you are and what you have to offer. You are the only person in the world who is like you. Your gifts are abundant and waiting to be heard.

Taking all these ideas to heart may change you and energize you to the degree that you can brush yourself off and start again, a crucial step in building your own resilience. Life presents many opportunities to believe in yourself and the world around you. The next time you find yourself struggling, tell yourself, "It's only change. I can deal with this."

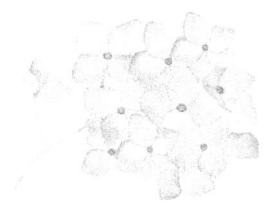

9

It's Just the Beginning

As I write and rewrite this final chapter, I finally acknowledge my resistance to bringing this book to an end. In keeping with my teachings, I asked myself the meaning of this behavior. From the beginning, this book has been an offer of love to those of you in search of acceptance and peace. In full disclosure, writing this book has been as much of a gift to me as it has been to anyone gaining even a grain of knowledge and comfort I hope to provide. I perceive it as a blessing to have been led to help others. I consider myself an instrument to be able to impart this knowledge at the right time to the right people, those who selected me to walk with them when in pain or grief. Now I realize that I needed to complete this task as much as my readers needed to believe in what is being said.

Throughout the chapters of this book you discovered the interlacing of a powerful premise. *Someone to Watch Over You* is all about *you*, the loving person you are meant to be, and your journey to find that person again. As you walk through life, things happen that create the chatter and ugliness that send you off course. There are far too many opportunities for others to define you when you fail to do this work yourself. You may need to let that go and dwell more on today and the many tomorrows that still hold opportunity for great joy. You can learn to love yourself even when you don't feel lovable. It is a mindset that requires a minute-to-minute approach of acceptance and patience with yourself and how life is unfolding. You may need to take risks but remember, even baby steps will provide you a new beginning.

Be your own best friend and seek out others who already find something wonderful about you. In your innocence, you arrived into this world a complete and lovable individual. You were like no other and very much who you were meant to be. You quickly learned and adapted to inherited traits and norms from the people around you. If fortunate enough, family served as the foundation from which you experienced safety and security. Their lessons of unconditional love were meant to provide the trust and confidence you needed in order to grow. However, if your parents were never taught how to love themselves, this lesson may not have been passed down to you either.

As you grew older, you learned all that you could about opinions, values, and beliefs that later served you on your life journey. You intuitively recognized the need to formulate your own engaging qualities in order to develop a life rich in relationships.

In the days, weeks, months, and years ahead of you, you will be challenged and even validated, but the most important action required is for you to love and accept the person you are becoming. Tomorrow morning when you look in the mirror, sing your praises and let yourself begin each day with a mantra that has meaning to you. Here's one to try if you feel called to it:

I love you for who you are. You move through life with purpose and bring joy to a world that sometimes struggles for peace. You are mindful to speak words of truth and kindness. You are a beacon of light. I love your passion to find beauty. I am always here with you to give you courage and strength for all the challenges you may face today. Your potential is great—now go out and put it to good use.

For those who had a rocky beginning, be comforted by the fact that you are hardly alone. It is never too late to find meaningful ways to love yourself and do the work to get you back on track. Embracing the person you are becoming requires acceptance and validation only *you* can provide. A great way to start is to purposely surround yourself with others who can help you continually refine the *self* you are meant to be. One way to do this is to affirm your present state as a starting point.

"In the infinity of life where I am, all is perfect, whole, and complete. I no longer choose to believe in old limitations and things I may be lacking. I now choose to begin to see myself as the Universe sees me, perfect, whole, and complete."[42]

—*Louise Hay*

When you suffer a grave loss to the integrity of *self*, you may perceive a part of you is missing, leaving you unstable and unsure. If there is a death or the death of a relationship, the loss of a job or home, you likely *are* missing the many parts and pieces that joined you to that person or place, all of which served to provide a sense of wholeness, an identity, purpose, and meaning. Perhaps, for the first time, you are coping with the fact that bad things can find you.

Finding Your Soul Friends

During this time, there are many lessons to learn. One important lesson includes building a safe, secure existence by exercising your ability to be responsible and accountable. To be successful in your transition to becoming your own person, you will be called upon to carefully discern all that is before you, to trust your own instincts, and to selectively trust the intuition of others. Creating a life that is surrounded by loving people who care about you will allow you to establish a meaningful group of "forever friends."

In writings dating back to the time of Plato and reappearing in Celtic philosophy, there is a belief that two souls with a unique connection are stronger together than they are apart. The Celts describe this as your *anam cara*, or "soul friend." The Celts believe that your *anam cara* can be a friend, companion, or spiritual guide.

Conceptually, *anam cara* supports the existence of your chosen people, those who last throughout your life. They also believe that everyone—either directly or on a more unconscious level—ultimately wants to find their one true soul mate. I am convinced there is more than one. These are the people in your life who remain "by your side" no matter the physical distance between you or the amount of time since you last spoke.

Much like the Paraclete discussed earlier in this book, your soul friends support you and sometimes mentor or teach you. They are not here to always agree with all you do or say but may be forthright and dependable in sharing their thoughts and opinions. They are not here to judge or sway you from a belief, but to help you see perspectives you may not see. Most of all, they love you for who you are.

At times, they may simply surround you with the joy they feel in being a part of your life. Your soul friends do not expect anything in return and may even place your success first to demonstrate the nature of a true relationship. These are the people in your life who do not require any conditional circumstances to encourage them to stay. When you think of them, you feel the same warm connection coming from deep inside of you as if suddenly, off in the distance, you see someone you love. The friendship is as comfortable as putting on an old pair of shoes that are worn, yet remain beautiful. Despite differences in your lifestyles or the fact that your paths took you in different directions, you return to one another with considerable ease.

My soul friends seem to be able to consider ways to explore needs without overstepping boundaries. Knowing we maintain busy schedules, we reach out by text, setting up time to talk by phone. When the effects of chemotherapy were at its worst, my dear friends left flowers and sweets at our doorstep and never once insisted to visit or call when this was not a possibility. One kindly friend made soup hoping that it would be something I could eat when my appetite returned. When a relationship is reciprocal, the best thing you can do to strengthen that bond is to find time to be together—one of the most valuable things a person can give of themselves.

I have learned throughout life that family, particularly siblings, may not always fill this role. In fact, many of my therapy clients went through life recognizing how different they were from their brothers and sisters. They often jokingly wondered whether they had been left on the doorstep of their home rather than being born into the family. If you have siblings, you are doubly fortunate to be related, but with all our humanity, siblings may have expectations that are different than what is expected in a soul friendship; they may act on unfinished business and envy instead of the purity that a soul friend provides.

Journal Exercise

Who Are Your Soul Friends?

Take a moment and consider who comes to mind when you think about a soul mate or a soul friend. Are there people who emerge in your life in times of need? Have you felt honored to be related to another person or persons? Is there someone you look up to, emulating their behavior and their response to crisis? Are you in search of your soul friends? What do you think you need in a friend? Do your best to name your soul friends here and provide some thoughts about your needs:

_____
_____
_____
_____
_____
_____
_____

Chapter 9: It's Just the Beginning

_____
_____
_____
_____
_____
_____
_____
_____
_____
_____
_____
_____
_____
_____
_____
_____
_____
_____

Speaking Your Truth

As you go through life, you may fail to take that extra moment to speak your truth to those people who casually enter your life, and especially to those who are most precious to you.

When I was diagnosed with cancer, I realized that every breath I took was an opportunity to tell those around me how I felt about them. Once I realized that life has a defined beginning and an end, I accepted the importance of speaking about love, and the value in clearing the air about anything that was standing in the way.

It is important for all of you to realize that life is not always predictable, but it surely has an end. Don't wait for the "right moment" or a "better opportunity" to live your life or find forgiveness and ways to clarify with the people you love. Time is precious. This may involve letting a friend or colleague know how much you appreciate all they do. It may be telling your spouse about the love you've experienced with them in your life. You may want to let your children know the pride they give you as they grow to be extraordinarily respectful and giving adults. You may want to praise someone's work ethic in getting the job done. And to your great surprise, when you finally push aside your own powerful denial system, you will teach others how to appreciate life.

It may be worth your consideration to reevaluate how to practice gratitude. We tend to spend so much time considering what we don't have that we miss the opportunity to be grateful for who we are and the many things and people that enrich our experience each day. There is exceptional value in every human encounter; treating it as though it will be your last may be another lesson that provides profound meaning.

Unfortunately, human beings too often fail to express themselves. It may appear as though you are taking others for granted or delaying the emotional investment it takes to be truthful. It takes effort to put thoughts and feelings into words and may seem easier to just walk away, storing the burden of anger or failing to express sentiments of kindness. As individuals, this hardens us and may set off a way of being and an existence that hardly lives up to our hopes and dreams.

Are you that person who avoids owing anything to anyone else and works diligently to always even the score when someone shows kindness? This may leave you wondering why you find yourself alone when you're hurting and need a friend. It is quite possible that these are the ground rules you established when you engineered your relationship boundaries. You tried hard to convince others that you are a capable human being and need no one. You may have remained in complicated relationships that wouldn't allow a deeper commitment, or perhaps you have been known to send people away, fearful of getting too close. Be sure to examine this phenomenon; it likely represents one of many relationship styles that may need to be revised. People often connect in magical ways, but when you admit to your needs and let another human being meet those needs, a wondrous experience unfolds. Remember, humans need to be needed.

I am the first to admit that once you're accustomed to a lifetime of refusals or failures, it's much more difficult to accept the fact that others may want to assist you with no strings attached. When working with couples and families in my therapy practice, a frequent pattern emerged between college-aged kids and their parents. I know because it happened to me. You raise your children to be independent and launch them into the world. You encourage them to be kind to others, productive, and successful in their relationships and the work they choose. All the while, you know the world can be bleak at times where demands place our emerging young at a disadvantage. The instinct is to protect, but you know full well that this action can be an obstacle to your child's development. It may even be interpreted that deep down you don't trust their ability or believe in them when you are actually hoping to avoid those skinned knees.

So, how should you respond to the desire to protect yet at the same time give them the best chance to grow? You do so with a deep faith that all that you have provided as a foundation truly works. This is a powerful example of a "both/and" situation and one where good communication becomes essential. With much respect for your child's ability, faith in the world, and an abundance of effective communication, it is important to let the child go. Yet at the same time, they need to know that you are always there in the background, cheering them on.

Parents also may have unmet needs once their children take flight. It may be that you were in a caring role with your children for some 20 years and suddenly that role has disappeared. You are now grieving the loss of that role. Even though there is a loss of *self* that needs to be filled, a goal for you could be to appreciate all that you have accomplished—a job well done. You also have needs that may be different now. For me, I need to know that my children are well and finding ways to enjoy life. I need to know when they are facing challenges and conflicts and how they are able to resolve these or not. I also need to know when they need our help and when they would prefer to take a risk on their own. A family value, if not already established, is to be able to state what you need without judgement or fear and to be able to problem-solve how to resolve those unmet needs.

If I haven't said it before, I want to emphasize the joy that each of you bring to the world. Some of you may have been doubting yourself yet in truth you have always been more than good enough. You arrived in this life with incredible potential. It was no accident that you persisted and managed to live through all that you did. Within you rests meaning and purpose, and there is no other person quite like you. Despite the burdens you experienced, you found ways to survive and often thrive. At times you give of yourself unselfishly, even escaping the notice of others who receive your help. You may feel as if you don't deserve help from others and asking for help may be alien to the relationships you've developed.

There will be seasons in your life when you will face adversity, some even that you yourself create. You may have times when you anguish over a decision, experience the loss of someone or something precious to you, or are facing the reality that your own personal health has set new limits to your life. The pain of loss can turn your attention away from your joy and replace it with a darkness that is unfamiliar and difficult to ignore.

Simply said, life offers experiences where you have choices. But these choices are not always black and white. In early stages of life, you are still developing your wisdom and sense of mastery. You're faced with many different perspectives to consider, and it takes a considerable amount of time and energy on your part. It's like trying on new clothes until you find the exact right size and style that suits you. (In truth, there may be many styles that you realize you can own and use in life.)

As you enter adulthood, your comfort with new experiences is quite contingent upon your success with experimenting life as a child and teenager. This includes the ability to fail and bounce back. If you were overprotected as a child, you may have been left to question your innate ability to make the right choice. Your parents may have tried to shield you in bubble wrap as it was their instinct to protect you from the outside world. While you won't always have all the answers or may not have had enough experience to safely provide yourself direction, there is always a benefit in trying. If you fall, pick yourself up and try again.

It is most important to remember that you have choice, a powerful ability to take action that provides the best possible outcome. Consider the fact that you would never intentionally go after the poorest choice; you will always try to make the best choice. It will be based on the wisdom, insight, and intuition you have gathered along the way. However, despite your best effort, there are times when circumstances are out of your control or you're missing vital information and the choice you make does not work in your favor. Such is life. Keep in mind that making a choice can be influenced by both the present conditions *and* your emotional state.

When making decisions, it's helpful to ask yourself if you're feeling any of the four basic feelings: Are you feeling glad, sad, mad, or scared? These feeling states might very well impact and unconsciously intrude on you making the best choice.

The strength within you will encourage you to find resilience. You will recall that resilience is a learned process that can help you during unexpected times. But resiliency only emerges when you determine who you want to be and how you want to respond to difficult situations. Remember you may be quite competent in certain parts of your life. Honor those parts while acknowledging your vulnerability in other parts. You may need to work on being open to accepting help when needed. It's just as important to work diligently to fill your life with loving people who can meet your needs in times of loss and support you in learning more about yourself. This is a gift for both of you.

At the same time, your job is to put your thoughts and feelings into words, not forcing others to guess who you are and what you need. You are the best judge of your ability to prosper. By demonstrating clarity, you can more easily and honestly use the skills that effectively teach you to be a self-reliant human being. This hardly means living a life alone but gives you the opportunity to live your life under your own guidance and with like-minded people who may be there to support you along the way. By gathering your strength from within while accepting the presence of others, you will live with intention, authenticity, and love in your heart.

We know that no man or woman is meant to be alone. We also believe that no one is meant to own us or take away our ability to stand free.

The best I can offer is an example from my own life.

In October of 2018, after three surgeries, a diagnosis of stage 3c metastatic ovarian cancer, and the prospect of only four years left to live, I began chemotherapy infusions as an outpatient. The course included pre-medication because of the potential side effects and then a combination of Taxol, Cisplatin, and Avastin. Each session took about six hours. I recall returning home with enough energy until noon the following day when the floor would fall out from under me. I became completely dependent. I referred to this time as "going to my dark place."

Each day I would get up from bed and attempt to shower before heading to the living room couch. I tried my best to spend time with my husband, who, like a deer in the headlights, worried over what he was seeing. He was a champion and patiently offered me choices to try to encourage me to eat. Every morning, he'd ask what I thought I could stomach, leave the house, and quickly return with bologna sandwiches, soup, or protein drinks. But there I stayed for about 10, sometimes 12 days, unable to talk or eat very much, only to repeat the process in another three weeks.

By January 2019, I had not eaten for 18 days. I never consciously gave up, yet I couldn't find a way to allow food to pass my lips. I was nauseous and had limited control over my bodily functions. This sedentary life contributed to the loss of considerable muscle mass and a decreased ability to walk. It was a Friday. I remember it clearly that the weekend was approaching, making it that much more difficult to speak with my oncologist. I called him and he sent me to the emergency room. As much as I didn't want to leave my home, I saw the fear on my husband's face as he worried that he wouldn't be able to provide me with the care I needed. I think we both knew I was dying before his eyes.

The next day after admission, I was beginning to prepare myself for an uncertain path. This time, even *I* was frightened. The Cancer Center chaplain came to see me. Tom gave me a blessing of the sick and I asked him to assure me that all my sins could be forgiven so that I could find heaven. He never asked further but reassured me that God was fully aware of who I was. I told Tom that with all the faith I always exercised, I couldn't find *myself*, the person who had been strong, the person everyone looked to for hope. Instead, I was planning to leave this life as I knew it.

With that, Tom made one last effort to enter my space by helping me visualize Jesus during his time of the Passion. This is part of Jesus' life when he was destined to address betrayal and accept death. Tom asked me to visualize myself in the Garden of Gethsemane where Jesus admitted to his Father his great sorrow and suffering. Because Tom knew my life was one of helping others, he asked me to seek out Jesus in the Garden and ask him *what he needed from me* to help him through this time. It was as though Tom intuitively knew to tap into a part of me that represented my spirit of giving, one that was far more comfortable than requesting help. As if touched by an angel, I found my way back where I could ask for guidance.[43]

People come into our lives just when we need them. Although you may find yourself amazed and humbled as I have on so many occasions, wisdom tells me that this is hardly a coincidence. If you are open—and hopefully you are—it may be time once again to look at all those who enter a space close enough to you. This doesn't mean the time you share with them is always a pleasant one. In fact, they may truly be a thorn in your side. Some stay for a length of time, while others leave us before we feel ready. Some individuals are here to teach you painful lessons that you may have resisted learning, while others are here to teach you something deeply perceptive about yourself or those around you.

For those seeking comfort and strength, I encourage you to explore all the possibilities to find untapped resources that may assist you in your journey. I turned to a higher power for strength, but know full well that for some, formalized religion may be a source of additional pain and discomfort. Resolving this hurt can be well worth the effort that one finds in a faith community. I had to step away from the religion I knew as a child to accept one that didn't impose guilt and instead offered new tangible opportunities to demonstrate acceptance. Remember, resolving hurt and old memories of anger can free you up to invite new people and experiences into your life that may bring you substantial joy and substance to move on to a better life.

Where will your search take you? Will you consider approaching people in a different manner? Will you seek out individuals from your past? Have you sometimes wondered what it would be like to be remembered?

Perhaps there are thoughts and feelings that were left unsaid or misunderstandings about moments that you shared. Have you played this over in your mind, wishing for a second chance now that you have greater clarity and the ability to communicate? Or, your wisdom may tell you that it is time to accept the reality of loss and to simply let go. And if you're struggling to find soul friends or a support system, you have tremendous advantages through technology and social media that can help you find a network of like-minded individuals.

Choosing You

In a quiet moment, when deep in solitude, have you ever asked what your life is all about? When we are born, we move from the safe space of our mother's womb to a life with a family and on to a larger community.

From the time I was very little, I can recall my feelings of gratitude to be born into *my* family, the one I have always cherished. I had loving parents and three siblings—all of whom were quite different from me. I had a sister who loved me as though I was her own, and in many ways, I think I was. We lived in a beautiful country that represented so many opportunities and freedoms. I remember praying for people so very far away who may not have had the advantages that were before me. I also realized that life wasn't always quite so simple and saw how the older and wiser adults around me were challenged by the complexities of life. Something inside told me that this life was going to be what I chose to make it.

No matter the pain or loneliness or new challenges heading in your direction, stop and take time to re-energize. Then, always choose *you*. It is you and only you who can come to terms with your life. Let me be clear about my message. I am not advocating that you take a deep dive under the covers and stay there. The bed is a place for rest, and, yes, you will need it as you come to terms with the loss and pain in your life.

You may be in physical pain, emotional pain, or both. Your spirit may be dwindling, and you may find it hard to see the path in front of you. But, somewhere deep inside is the loving individual who agreed to find a way to heal. You don't like feeling this way and, as in times before, it will take courage and stepping into the unknown to come out of this lonely place. I am here with you and know full well this walk can be lonely. I also know that it is up to us to decide how we choose to live this life until there is no more life to live. Because of you and the many people facing struggles around us, let's choose the path of love.

Journal Exercises

Ask yourself: Who are you at this moment in time?

Identify and characterize every part of you—including your emotional, physical, financial, and social state. Evaluate and prioritize each of these parts, knowing you may need to begin with one correction at a time. Be honest. Perhaps you are frightened and insecure because you have overextended your spending, which can be a symptom of seeking happiness in the wrong place. Or, is there something about the way you look that misrepresents the person you hope to project? Has your grief gotten in the way of caring about your personal hygiene or efforts to improve your appearance? Have you lost all order to even the simple things in life?

Emotional Status _____

_____

_____

_____

_____

Physical Status _____
_____
_____
_____
_____
_____

Financial Status _____
_____
_____
_____
_____
_____

Social Status _____
_____
_____
_____
_____
_____

Ask yourself: Who do you truly want to be?

If you know the answer to this question, congratulate yourself. If not, describe a time when you were truly happy. What might be missing now that does not provide the same kind of happiness? Is there something inside you that you aren't sure of? For example, if you see yourself as a loving human being, what do people see when they meet you? Is there evidence of anger and resentment getting in your way? Have you become accustomed to defending yourself so that you treat all people as a source of danger? Do you project a certain attitude that is unbecoming or self-defeating? _____
_____
_____
_____
_____
_____

Ask yourself: How can you invite forgiveness into your life?

Are there circumstances from your past that require your forgiveness? One by one, identify the person or persons involved in any past hurts. When did that begin? How come? Are there people in your life who need to be forgiven? If you accept that each of us holds responsibility for our experiences in life, is it possible you contributed to this yourself? If so, now is the time to forgive yourself.

_____
_____
_____
_____
_____
_____
_____
_____

Ask yourself: What steps do you need to take to reach your goals?

Try your best to get in touch with any thoughts and feelings that get in your way. If it's anger, then steps may need to be taken toward forgiveness. Start with a careful and honest review of the circumstances that stimulate your anger, your fear, or your awareness of hurt. It might help to do a cognitive shift in order to view the event from the eyes of other individuals involved. You may then need to let go or redefine the importance of the event so that it no longer controls you.

_____
_____
_____
_____
_____
_____
_____
_____

Ask yourself: What moments have taken your breath away?

To quote Maya Angelou, "Life is not measured by the number of breaths we take, but by the moments that take our breath away." What are these moments for you? What did you feel then? What do you feel now, remembering it all? Write down these moments below. I hope you run out of space.

_____
_____
_____
_____
_____
_____
_____
_____
_____
_____
_____
_____
_____
_____
_____
_____
_____
_____
_____
_____

If all else fails:

Remember, love exists above you, below you, and beside you. Every day at least one person in this world thinks about you in a loving way. If you have a friend whom you cherish, let them know how you feel. It's not too late to repair your bridges and let down your guard. Let people in and have the confidence to know that you are better prepared to deal with whatever comes your way. Be sure to love and forgive yourself no matter what.

And most of all…

Chapter 9: It's Just the Beginning

Be Not Afraid

You shall cross the barren desert, but you shall not die of thirst.
You shall wander far in safety, though you do not know the way.
You shall speak your words in foreign lands, and all will understand,
You shall see the face of God and live.

Be not afraid, I go before you always, come follow Me,
and I shall give you rest.

If you pass through raging waters in the sea, you shall not drown.
If you walk amidst the burning flames, you shall not be harmed.
If you stand before the power of hell and death is at your side,
know that I am with you, through it all.

Be not afraid, I go before you always, come follow Me,
and I shall give you rest.

Blessed are your poor, for the Kingdom shall be theirs.
Blessed are you that weep and mourn, for one day you shall laugh.
And if wicked men insult and hate you, all because of Me,
blessed, blessed are you!

Be not afraid, I go before you always, come follow Me,
and I shall give you rest.[44]

My Many Thanks

As indicated throughout the pages of this book, my journey began with many blessings—including the ability to receive and make good use of an education that forever allows me the privilege to make a difference in the lives of others. I could not have had any success without the loving people who filled my life each step of the way. Blessings multiplied just when I needed support to get through the years of care after being diagnosed with cancer. I am here and ultimately able to fulfill a personal legacy: The joy of writing this book. I hold a special place for every one of you who have walked beside me.

For those I have yet to meet, *Someone to Watch Over You: Finding Your Strength Within* carries a message. When all is said and done, you have yourself to rely on. Use all of your engaging qualities wisely. Find strength to heal. Believe in yourself. Fill your life with loving people. You are deserving and you are enough.

To my husband George: My life became more than I ever imagined the day you appeared. I know you didn't always have my vision, but you believed in me and what I hoped could be possible. This gave me the courage to go on, even when it would have been easier to give up. I love you more!

To my children Christopher and Michael: Thank you so much for the joy you brought to our lives and for completing our miracle. As adults, your love expanded our family to our daughters-in-law Jordan and Heather, and the added distinction of being "Mema" and "Pop Pop" to our dear grandchildren, Ruby and Charlie.

Thank you to my wonderful sister Carole who helped me see the world, brothers Bobby and Richard, sisters-in-law Dottie, Dorothy and Judy, cousins Janice, Teddy, and Hanette, and Aunt Gilda who have been checking in with me and offering their incredible support.

Thank you to my nursing staff at Pardee Hospital during my time as their director and more recently when I became someone under their care. Thank you, Bridget, Lynne, Renee, Leann, Cheryl, and Deana, Dr. Radford, my oncologist, and Drs. Phelps, Glassman, Byrd, and Beaty, all of whom work to keep me alive today. A special thanks to Tom Vallie who took me through the Garden of Gethsemane. You saved me.

Thank you to Penn State Health and e4 for allowing me to end my consulting career on an incredibly high note. To my colleagues Lisa, Steve, Ann, Jim F., Jill, and Kimberly.

To my Soul Friends: Those of you who entered my life as early as first grade and managed to remain present through time and space. Thank you to Pammie, Beverly, Bonnie and Bob, Carri and Cliff, Jeff and Julie, Barbara, Geri, and Charles.

About the Author

Ellen J. Reed, MBA, MSN, RN, PMHCNS-BC is an advanced practice nurse, specializing in psychobehavioral aspects of the adult. Her advanced degrees and certifications support her competence to treat clients in multiple practice settings with a particular focus on relationships, self-awareness, change, and experiences related to loss.

For 10 years, Ellen served as a clinical nurse specialist/psychiatric consultation liaison nurse for Robert Wood Johnson University Hospital in New Brunswick, New Jersey. While there, she was referred by physicians and nurses to intervene with patients and families facing traumatic and progressive illnesses in one of their many critical care units and their Cancer Center. Ellen also addressed the extreme stress in providing care or being a caregiver when hope for improvement was not likely.

Ellen created a private practice using Grief and Loss, Nursing, and Gestalt Theory as a foundation where she encouraged clients to address issues by honoring their past while owning their present. She advocated the benefit of being in touch with both thoughts and feelings, with the understanding that many areas of discontent relate back to unfinished business and unresolved grief.

Throughout her years as a therapist, Ellen recognized the incredible stress individuals experienced in their respective work settings or in times of critical life change. She developed an understanding of the phenomena surrounding members of the workforce and their leaders and continues to foster experiences to alleviate stress through more meaningful communication. This can be especially profound for participants who need a safe place to acknowledge the pain associated with being present to those who are suffering.

Later, Ellen served as a nursing director for Pardee Hospital, now Pardee UNC Health Care, in Western North Carolina where she provided oversight to approximately 120 nursing staff members and physicians. She acted as a visionary, supporting and advancing the work of the Comprehensive Community Cancer service teams, Regional Behavioral Health Services, and Women and Children's Health. Her premise was always to foster autonomy and encourage people to stretch beyond their comfort level in order to promote growth in themselves and in their organization.

Ultimately, she became a consultant to integrate her work on a corporate level to hospitals throughout the nation as they embraced standardization and documentation of practice. With a primary focus on improving the quality of care for patients, it was in this realm where she identified the value in influencing culture and served as a role model for direct, timely, and open communication. Ellen has always insisted that promoting the awareness of individual perceptions, feelings, and cognitive functions has consistently enhanced positive outcomes, especially when colleagues were given clear direction and expectations, and when their contribution to the whole truly mattered.

Having had a wealth of anecdotal and empirical evidence supporting her influence in the growth of clients and staff, Ellen's lifelong dream has been to write a book that could touch the hearts and minds of many more people who search for an opportunity to reach greater peace.

Ellen now lives in Western North Carolina with her amazing husband of 38 years. She is mother to Christopher Andrew Reed and Michael Thomas Reed, mother-in-law to two amazing daughters-in-law Heather and Jordan Reed, and "Mema" to two grandchildren Ruby and Charlie Reed.

Notes

Intent:
1. The Reverend Tim Jones, Sermon. St. James Episcopal Church, Hendersonville, NC, May 25, 2019.

Who Should Read This Book:
2. Johnson, Barry. *Polarity Management: Recognizing and Solving Unsolvable Problems*, 2nd edition. Amherst, MA: HRD Press, Inc., 1996.

Chapter 1:
3. Covey, Stephen R. *The 7 Habits of Highly Effective People: Powerful Lessons in Personal Change*. New York: Free Press, 2004.
4. McGraw, Phil, PhD. "The Dr. Phil Show." October 22, 2019.
5. Prather, Hugh. *Notes to Myself: My Struggle to Become a Person*. Designed by M' NO Productions, Inc. London: Penguin Random House, 1983.
6. Ochsner, Kevin. Columbia University citation from research presented at the NeuroLeadership Summit. Boston, 2018.
7. Maslow, A. H. *A Theory of Human Motivation*. Psychological Review, 50(4), pp. 370-396. Oregon: Rough Draft Printing, 2013 (reprint of 1943 edition). This material is in the public domain.
8. Sullivan, Harry. *The Interpersonal Theory of Psychiatry*. New York: W.W. Norton & Co., 1953.
9. Maslow, A. H. *A Theory of Human Motivation*. Psychological Review, 50(4), pp. 370-396. Oregon: Rough Draft Printing, 2013 (reprint of 1943 edition). This material is in the public domain.
10. Heffron, Jack. *The Writer's Idea Book*. Ohio: Writer's Digest Books, 2000.

Chapter 2:
11. Luft, J. and Ingham, H. *The Johari Window, a Graphic Model of Interpersonal Awareness*. Proceedings of the western training laboratory in group development. Los Angeles: University of California, Los Angeles, 1955.
12. Reed, Jordan. "How to Practice Non-Attachment When Close Friends Move Away," *Shut Up and Yoga*. https://shutupandyoga.com, 2019.

13. Luft, J. and Ingham, H. *The Johari Window, a Graphic Model of Interpersonal Awareness. Proceedings of the western training laboratory in group development.* Los Angeles: University of California, Los Angeles, 1955.
14. Galatians, Chapter 6:7. The King James Bible.

Chapter 3:

15. McLeod, S. A. Jean *Piaget's Theory of Cognitive Development.* Simply Psychology. https://www.simplypsychology.org/piaget.html, June 6, 2018.
16. Pew Research Center. "Millennials: A Portrait of Generation Next." https://www.pewresearch.org/wp-content/uploads/sites/3/2010/10/millennials-confident-connected-open-to-change.pdf.
17. United States Census Bureau Report, 2020.
18. Russo, Susan. *Savoring Memories of Sunday Dinner.* NPR's "Kitchen Window." December 12, 2007.

Chapter 4:

19. Dickens, Charles. *A Tale of Two Cities.* London: Chapman & Hall, 1859.
20. Heinz, Kate. *13 Signs of a Bad Company Culture and How to Improve.* BuiltIn.com, December 12, 2019.

Chapter 5:

21. Sherrick, Clarence. "How Would You Define Love?" Quora, https://www.quora.com/How-would-you-define-love-3. November 14, 2014.
22. 1 Corinthians, Chapter 13: 4-7. New International Version (NIV).
23. Nepo, Mark. *The Book of Awakening: Having the Life You Want by Being Present to the Life You Have* (Gift Edition). San Francisco: Conari Press, 2011.
24. Gorman, Michele. "Gay Marriage is Legal in All 50 States: Supreme Court." Newsweek, June 26, 2015.

Chapter 6:

25. Floyd, Kory, Ph.D. *Seven Reasons to Be More Physically Affectionate.* Psychology Today: September 27, 2013.
26. Sullivan, Harry. *The Interpersonal Theory of Psychiatry.* New York: W.W. Norton & Co., 1953.

27. Yates, James. "My Three Dogs." Training document provided with permission. 2020.
28. Luft, Joseph & Harrington, Ingham. *The Johari Window: A Graphic Model of Interpersonal Awareness.* Proceedings of the Western Training Laboratory in Group Development. Los Angeles: University of California, Los Angeles, 1955.
29. All names referring to clients or people with whom I worked with have been changed to maintain anonymity.
30. Myers, Gail & Myers, Michele. *The Dynamics of Human Communication: A Laboratory Approach, 6th ed.* New York: McGraw-Hill Humanities/Social Sciences/Languages, 1991.
31. Luft, Joseph & Harrington, Ingham. *The Johari Window: A Graphic Model of Interpersonal Awareness.* Proceedings of the Western Training Laboratory in Group Development. Los Angeles: University of California, Los Angeles, 1955.
32. Patterson, Kerry, Grenny, Joseph, McMillan, Ron, & Switzler, Al. "Crucial Conversations: Tools for Talking When Stakes are High." New York: McGraw-Hill Education, 2001.

Chapter 7:

33. Pert, Candace. *Molecules of Emotion: The Science Behind Mind-Body Medicine.* New York: Touchstone Edition, 1999.
34. Upledger, John E. *Your Inner Physician and You: CranioSacral Therapy and SomatoEmotional Release.* California: North Atlantic Books, 1992.
35. Ecclesiastes 3:1-8. New Kings James Version.

Chapter 8:

36. Frankl, Viktor E. *Man's Search for Meaning.* Boston: Beacon Press, 2006.
37. American Psychiatric Association. *Diagnostic and Statistical Manual of Mental Disorders, 5th Edition*: DSM-5. 2013.
38. Titelman, Gregory Y. *Random House Dictionary of Popular Proverbs and Sayings.* New York: Random House, 1996.
39. Norris, Fran. "How we Bounce Back: The New Science of Human Resilience." World Science Festival, New York, May 31, 2012.
40. Holmes, Thomas and Rahe, Richard. "The Social Readjustment Rating Scale." Journal of Psychosomatic Research, Vol. 11, Issue 2, Pages 213-218. Amsterdam: Elsevier Science, Inc., August

1967. All rights reserved. With permission from Elsevier [License Number 4796561134219].

41. Shakespeare, William. *The Merry Wives of Windsor*. 1602.

Chapter 9:

42. Hay, Louise. *You Can Heal Your Life*. Carlsbad: Hay House, Inc.: 1984.
43. Vallie, Tom. "Praying the Passion with Jesus." January 11, 2019. (Inspired by Hebert, Yvonne's *Finding Peace in Pain*. Living Flame Press, 1984.)
44. St. Louis Jesuits & Bob Dufford, S.J. *Be Not Afraid*. https://www.youtube.com/watch?v=snmwD6d9Xo4

Recommended Reading

1. Boszormenyi-Nagy, Ivan, and Framo, James. *Intensive Family Therapy: Theoretical and Practical Aspects*. New York: Routledge Taylor and France Group, 1985.
2. Graham, Linda. *Resilience: Powerful Practices for Bouncing Back from Disappointment, Difficulty, and Even Disaster*. Novato, California: New World Library, 2018.
3. Heffron, Jack. *The Writer's Idea Book: How to Develop Great Ideas for Fiction, Non-Fiction, Poetry, and Screenplays*. Ohio: Writer's Digest Books, 2011.
4. Housden, Roger. *Ten Poems to Say Goodbye,* New York: Harmony Books, 2012.
5. Kalanithi, Paul. When Breath Becomes Air. New York: Random House, 2016.
6. Myers, Gail & Myers, Michele. *The Dynamics of Human Communication: A Laboratory Approach, 6th ed*. New York: McGraw-Hill Humanities/Social Sciences/Languages, 1991.
7. Nelson, Thomas. *New King James Version of the Holy Bible*. Grand Rapids, Michigan: HarperCollins Christian Publishing, Zondervan Division, 1982.
8. Nouwen, Henri. *Bread for the Journey: A Daybook of Wisdom and Faith*. New York: HarperCollins, 1997.
9. O'Donohue, John. *Anam Cara: A Book of Celtic Wisdom*. New York: Harper Perennial, 2004.
10. Oliver, Mary. *Felicity*. New York: Penguin Books, 2015.

11. Prather, Hugh. *Notes to Myself: My Struggle to Become a Person.* Designed by M' NO Productions, Inc. London: Penguin Random House, 1983.
12. Sanders, C.M. *Grief: The Mourning After, Dealing with Adult Bereavement.* New York: John Wiley and Sons, 1989.
13. Stedeford, Averil. *Facing Death: Patients, Families, and Professionals.* London: William Heinemann Medical Books Ltd., 1985.
14. Worden, J.W. *Grief Counseling and Grief Therapy: A Handbook for the Mental Health Practitioner.* New York: Springer, 1982.

www.ingramcontent.com/pod-product-compliance
Lightning Source LLC
Chambersburg PA
CBHW071313110426
42743CB00042B/1431